Distinguished Wisdom Presents . . .
"Living Proverbs"—Vol. 1

—*Over 500 Wisdom Nuggets
To Enrich Your Life*—

Pastor Terrance Levise Turner, MBA

Well Spoken Inc.| *Nashville, TN*

© 2018 Terrance Levise Turner

All rights reserved. No part of this publication may be reproduced, scanned, transmitted or distributed in any printed or electronic or mechanical forms or methods, including photocopying, recording, or other without prior written permission of the publisher, except in the case of brief select quotations embodied in critical reviews and certain other noncommercial uses permitted by copyright law. For permission requests, write to the publisher, addressed below.

Unless otherwise indicated, all Scripture quotations are taken from the King James Version of the Bible. Unless otherwise indicated all original quotes are those of
Pastor Terrance Levise Turner.

Well Spoken Inc.
P.O. Box 291806 Nashville, TN. 37229
WellSpokenInc@bellsouth.net
www.TerranceTurnerBooks.com

Ordering Information

Quantity sales. Special discounts are available on quantity purchases by corporations, associations, and others. For details, contact the "Special Sales Department" at the address above.

Cover design by Ryan Urz/Susan of LSDdesign/99Designs.com
Book design by Terrance L. Turner

Printed in the United States of America

ISBN	9780999323632	and	9780999323663	paperback
ISBN	9780999323649	and	9780999323670	hardcover
ISBN	9780999323656	and	9780999323687	Ebook

This book is dedicated to young people of today and of future generations. I desire that they have a solid understanding of God and His principles for life and thereby have a successful, prosperous, safe, and godly life.

Contents

Acknowledgements VII
Preface XI
Introduction XIII
"Living Proverbs"-Vol.1 1
Final Word 185
About The Author 186

Acknowledgements

I would like to acknowledge the enduring love and support of my wife, Dr. Avis Turner for all of the dedication, understanding, and sacrifice that she has given to me during our years of marriage. Her love and devotion is an unmerited gift from God that has allowed me to remain focused to achieve God's best for our lives.

Thank you to my mother, Geraldine Key. She is the foundation of my life, faith, and character. My mother committed to loving my brothers and me by teaching us to know and reverence God as our heavenly Father and Jesus Christ as our Lord and Savior. Her sacrifice and dedication to the ways of God are the reasons I have become dedicated to God as my Father.

The wisdom that I gained from my mother, Geraldine Key, grandmother, Wilma Starks, and grandfather, Clarence Young became the foundation for being able to successfully navigate life. "Wisdom is the principle thing." (Proverbs 4:7) Thank God for the faithful people He put in my life as sources of wisdom

Preface

My mother introduced my brothers and me to God as our Father by teaching us the principles of the book of Proverbs in the Bible. She sat down with us in Bible studies and prayer and taught us the principles of morality, godliness, and wisdom for life that the Book of Proverbs contained. She took us to church, and she lived the principles of God's Word before us in our home. My mother's dedication to the Lord Jesus Christ was my example for seeing how to live a life sanctified unto God. Through her example, along with my grandmother's, I gained a deep love for God and His principles.

     As I grew up and became an adult, I continued to look to God's Word as the source of wisdom for life. The book of Proverbs became my mainstay of reliable wisdom. The structure of the book and the manner in which the truths were conveyed were easy for me to digest. They are direct, bite-sized, concentrated nuggets of truth. This affected and helped to craft and shape my thinking.

Distinguished Wisdom Presents: Living Proverbs — Vol. 1 came into being gradually, day by day, as a result of sharing wisdom nuggets as posts with friends on social media. God led me to begin sharing the wisdom I had learned and ascertained from walking with Him with others who could be enlightened and encouraged by what was offered.

Living Proverbs came into being in real time as I was led by the Spirit and shared with others what I believed would minister to their lives. My prayer is that they will minister to you now and in time to come.

Pastor Terrance Levise Turner

Introduction

Historical Aspects of Biblical Proverbs

First Kings 3:4–14 gives the account of King Solomon becoming king after his father, King David, died. He, though a full grown man, felt as if he was a child in regards to taking over such an immense responsibility to reign as king, especially after such a notable mark his father had made on the kingdom of Israel and history.

Solomon prayed to God for wisdom to rule justly and with good understanding for God's people. The following passage describes the account:

> And the king went to Gibeon to sacrifice there; for that was the great high place: a thousand burnt offerings did Solomon offer upon that altar. In Gibeon the Lord appeared to Solomon in a dream by night: and God said, Ask what I shall give thee. And Solomon said, Thou hast shewed unto thy servant David my father great mercy, according as he walked before thee in truth, and in righteousness, and in uprightness of heart with thee; and thou hast kept for him this great kindness, that thou hast given him a son to sit on his throne, as it is this day. And now, O Lord my God, thou hast made thy servant king instead of David my

father: and I am but a little child: I know not how to go out or come in. And thy servant is in the midst of thy people which thou hast chosen, a great people, that cannot be numbered nor counted for multitude.

Give therefore thy servant an understanding heart to judge thy people, that I may discern between good and bad: for who is able to judge this thy so great a people? And the speech pleased the Lord, that Solomon had asked this thing. And God said unto him, Because thou hast asked this thing, and hast not asked for thyself long life; neither hast asked riches for thyself, nor hast asked the life of thine enemies; but hast asked for thyself understanding to discern judgment;

Behold, I have done according to thy words: lo, I have given thee a wise and an understanding heart; so that there was none like thee before thee, neither after thee shall any arise like unto thee.

And I have also given thee that which thou hast not asked, both riches, and honour: so that there shall not be any among the kings like unto thee all thy days. And if thou wilt walk in my ways, to keep my statutes and my commandments, as thy father David did walk, then I will lengthen thy days. (1 Kings 3:4–14)

We see that God gave King Solomon wisdom to reign over His people, unlike any other king. The wisdom Solomon obtained, was the key to great riches, honor, and renown.

Solomon was a teacher. He was a preacher as well. He taught his sons and others his wisdom using proverbs, parables, and wise sayings. He felt that this was the best way to help those that heard his wisdom to understand the concepts he was attempting to convey.

In Ecclesiastes 1:1 King Solomon calls himself "the Preacher." This is what it says:

> The words of the Preacher, the son of David, king in Jerusalem.

The book of Proverbs also gives us the biblical purpose of using proverbs, parables, and wise sayings to teach. Proverbs 1:1–7 defines the purpose of the Book of Proverbs, as well as the purpose of this book *Living Proverbs*:

> The proverbs of Solomon the son of David, king of Israel; To *know* wisdom and instruction; to *perceive* the words of understanding; To *receive* the instruction of wisdom, justice, and judgment, and equity; To give *subtlety* to the simple, to the young man knowledge and discretion. A wise man will hear, and will increase learning; and a man of understanding shall attain unto wise counsels: To *understand* a proverb, and the *interpretation*; the words of the wise, and their dark sayings. The fear of the Lord is the beginning of knowledge: but fools despise wisdom and instruction.
> (Proverbs 1:1–7)

Notice that I emphasized a few key words in this passage of Scripture, which I would like to point out to you;

they clearly explain the purpose of the biblical Book of Proverbs, as well as this book.

The first word I would like to point out is the word *know*. *The Strong's Exhaustive Concordance of the Bible* defines this word like this:

3045– yada

1. to know or ascertain by seeing

2. observation, recognition, instruction

3. acknowledge, acquainted with

4. to know assuredly

5. to be aware

6. to know for a certainty

7. to cause to discern

8. to discover

Therefore, based on these definitions, we see that the initial purpose of biblical proverbs is so the reader may know and ascertain God's wisdom by clearly seeing it. It is to allow the person to observe the deeper meaning of a subject in a condensed way. It is to teach the person how to recognize wisdom when it is being spoken and to take heed to instruction when it is being given.

The speaking of proverbs is a way of conveying meaning that has been tested and tried as true. It is a way of conveying those truths to others in a condensed manner that they can gain the certainty of those truths.

They are given so people can discern truth when it is being presented, without having to have a full explanation. They will not have to have a full explanation in order to discern the meaning that is being conveyed.

Proverbs are a condensed conveying of deeper meaning.

The next word King Solomon uses to define the purpose of biblical proverbs is *perceive*. This is how the concordance defines it:

995–**biyn**

1. To separate mentally or to distinguish

2. understand

3. discern

4. be cunning

5. diligently

6. direct

7. to have intelligence

8. deal wisely

Notice the words used to define *perceive* are words that deal with the mind. One of the purposes of proverbs of all kinds is for the reader to become more keen in his or her thinking and thus, more capable to be successful in life.

The goal is for the person who heeds proverbs to learn to perceive and understand God's ways of doing and being right in life. It is that they will learn to discern right and wrong, as well as the timing and manner of doing the right thing.

Through studying proverbs, a young person, as well as those more experienced in life, will become more cunning or skillful in navigating decisions, people skills, etc. Various proverbs are given to encourage the reader to become more diligent in life matters and thus more successful and prosperous.

Short wise sayings, parables, and proverbs can provide swift guidance to a person's decision making. They will direct a person's steps in the midst of a decision– making process.

Through heeding various godly proverbs, a person will gain quick intelligence for good judgment. People who give themselves to proverbs as a companion to their lives will learn to deal wisely in life's diverse situations.

As people give themselves to the study of proverbs, they will learn to receive wisdom when it is being presented. They will gain more subtlety in life. They will become more discreet and refined in behavior and decision–making and

manner, thus making them better able to smoothly navigate the potentially rough matters of human relationships.

Ultimately, the biblical book of Proverbs, as well as this book, *Living Proverbs,* is written so that the person that heeds them may gain a greater understanding of God's principles for successful living and will be able to interpret God's wisdom as it is presented to him or her, whether through reading the Bible or in the lessons of life.

This is the purpose of this book *Living Proverbs.* My goal in writing this book is to convey the understanding of the Word of God and God's principles in such a way that it is easy for anyone to understand. My goal is to bring God's Word alive to your understanding.

What Is Wisdom?

What is wisdom? Why is it important? How is it obtained? How is it used?

These are all questions that I will answer for you in this book. Proverbs 4: 5–7 says:

> Get wisdom, get understanding: forget it not; neither decline from the words of my mouth. Forsake her not, and she shall preserve thee: love her, and she shall keep thee. Wisdom is the principle thing; therefore, get wisdom; and with all thy getting get understanding.

Therefore, we see that the wisdom of God is the number one, most vital thing we all need in order to live a successful life.

The following Scriptures further emphasize the vital importance of wisdom:

> The fear of the Lord is the beginning of knowledge: but fools despise wisdom and instruction. (Proverbs 1:7)

> Also, that the soul be without knowledge, it is not good; and he that hasteth with the feet sinneth. (Proverbs 19:2)

> He that getteth wisdom loveth his own soul: he that keepeth understanding shall find good. (Proverbs 19:8)

Based on these Scriptures, we can see that God's wisdom is vital for successful living. The name of this book is *Distinguished Wisdom Presents: Living Proverbs —Volume 1* because we must apply God's Word to our daily living for it to be beneficial to us.

Habakkuk 2:4b says, "The just shall live by his faith." In other words, the only way the faith and wisdom of the Word of God will work for us is when we actually live by what we learn. As God's Word is lived out in our daily life, it becomes wisdom gained by experience. We are then able to know with certainty the reliability of God's Word. We can then pass that wisdom on to our family, our friends, and those we come in contact with in our daily life.

Wisdom is for success in daily living. These *Living Proverbs* came forth out of my life of seeking to live by God's Word daily. I have dealt with the same challenges that many of you that read this book have had, and I have discovered that *God's Word works for those who work it.*

Please enjoy this book as a continual companion of counsel and guidance. All of the *Living Proverbs* are supported clearly by scriptural references. You will be able to have a relevant Bible study with every one of them. Meditate on them. Use it as a reference book. With every page you will find a nugget of wisdom that will enrich your daily life.

Now delve into the wisdom of God in *Distinguished Wisdom Presents: Living Proverbs—Volume 1.*

May Your Life Be Enriched By The Words Of Wisdom!

—Pastor Terrance Levise Turner

XXIII

"Living Proverbs"-Vol.1

1. If you don't respect the process, you won't respect the marriage.

Marriage is honorable in all, and the bed undefiled: but whoremongers and adulterers God will judge.

– Hebrews 13:4

2. Don't fight change. A changing life is a living life. The only people that don't change are the dead.

For to him that is joined to all the living there is hope: for a living dog is better than a dead lion.

– Ecclesiastes 9: 4

3. School is a refinery, but God puts the gold in the ground.

The fining pot is for silver, and the furnace for gold: but the Lord trieth the hearts.

– Proverbs 17: 3

4. Everyday is an exercise of choice. God Himself doesn't take your power of choice away. The Bible is an instruction manual of promises and examples for making the right choice. It also informs us of the consequences for making the wrong

choice. Yet, God Himself still doesn't take your power of choice away. It is the right of personhood.

I call heaven and earth to record this day against you, that I have set before you life and death, blessing and cursing: therefore choose life, that both thou and thy seed may live:

–Deuteronomy 30:19

5. Hurry, worry, and anxiety are clear indicators that your life's priorities are out of alignment.

And Jesus answered and said unto her, Martha, Martha, you are careful and troubled about many things: But one thing is needful: and Mary has chosen that good part, which shall not be taken away from her.

–Luke 10:41–42

6. Victory loves company!

He that walketh with wise men shall be wise: but a companion of fools shall be destroyed.

–Proverbs 13:20

7. Your success is not licensed by a degree or limited to a degree. A degree is only a tool for more intelligently utilizing your God-given talents.

Also, that the soul be without knowledge, it is not good; and he that hasteth with the feet sinneth.

– Proverbs 19:2

8. Don't be so anxious to run out on the field of life each day without reading the playbook—the Bible.

And Jesus answered him, saying, It is written, That man shall not live by bread alone, but by every word of God.

– Luke 4:4

9. A wise old owl sat on an oak.
The more he saw, the less he spoke.
The less he spoke, the more he heard.
 Why can't we be like that wise old bird?

–Anonymous

Wherefore, my beloved brethren, let every man be swift to hear, slow to speak, slow to wrath.

– James 1:19

10. See no evil. Hear no evil. Speak no evil. This is a key to focus when surrounded by foolish people. (Feeding your ears with something positive through some earphones helps too!)

Keep thy heart with all diligence; for out of it are the issues of life. Put away from thee a froward mouth, and perverse lips put far from thee. Let thine eyes look right on, and let thine eyelids look straight before thee. Ponder the path of thy feet, and let all thy ways be established . Turn not to the right hand nor to the left: remove thy foot from evil.

–Proverbs 4:23–27

11. There are certain general uncompromising guidelines regarding marriage. However, each married couple must eventually find their individual rhythm to make it work.

And he answered and said unto them, Have ye not read, that he which made them at the beginning made them male and female. And said, For this cause shall a man leave father and mother, and shall cleave to his wife: and they twain shall be one flesh? Wherefore they are no more twain, but one flesh. What therefore God hath joined together, let not man put asunder.

– Matthew 19:4–6

12. No matter what disappointments you may have experienced in life, and no matter what type of delays you may have had, if you put your hand in the hand of Jesus, God always has a way to lead you to a happy ending.

For our light affliction, which is but for a moment, works for us a far more exceeding weight of glory.

–2 Corinthians 4:17

13. True love, which is the God kind of love, never truly changes in its essence. It's like water. Water is H_2O. Period. It can change forms. It can be strong, cold, and solid. It can be hot, liquid, and boiling. It can become light and effervescent as droplets of evaporated steam. However, the true essence is always still H_2O. The God kind of love may have to take diverse forms to be effective, but in the final analysis, if it was ever true love, its essence will never change.

And now abideth faith, hope, charity, these three; but the greatest of these is charity.

–1 Corinthians 13:13

14. Anytime you seek to manifest excellence and divinity, the Devil will always attack you through someone else's carnality.

Because the carnal mind is enmity against God: for it is not subject to the law of God, neither indeed can be.

–Romans 8:7

15. We must often take the time to seek the Lord until we get down to the ground floor of our lives in order to truly see where we stand.

Seek ye The Lord while He may be found, call ye upon Him while He is near:

– Isaiah 55:6

16. Prayer is the highlight of the day!

And in the morning, rising up a great while before day, he went out, and departed into a solitary place, and there prayed.

– Mark 1:35

17. Don't make the rational or expedient decision. Make the effective, immediate decision that the prevailing condition requires.

And there came a voice to him, Rise, Peter; kill, and eat. But Peter said, Not so, Lord; for I have never eaten any thing that is common

or unclean. And the voice spake unto him again the second time, What God hath cleansed, that call not thou common.

– Acts 10:13–15

18. There are two rules for helping people: Help them with a hand up. Help them with a ladder. A hand up provides support, and a ladder provides tools for change and the steps to get there.

Now Peter and John went up together into the temple at the hour of prayer, being the ninth hour. And a certain man lame from his mother's womb was carried, whom they laid daily at the gate of the temple which is called Beautiful, to ask alms of them that entered into the temple; who seeing Peter and John about to go into the temple asked an alms. And Peter, fastening his eyes upon him with John, said, Look on us. And he gave heed unto them, expecting to receive something of them. Then Peter said, Silver and gold have I none; but such as I have give I thee: In the name of Jesus Christ of Nazareth rise up and walk. And he took him by the right hand, and lifted him up: and immediately his feet and ankle bones received strength. And he leaping up stood, and walked, and entered with them into the temple, walking, and leaping, and praising God.

– Acts 3:1–8

19. Look at what you are doing, not at what you are feeling, to determine your righteousness before God. Jesus made us righteous through His precious blood; it's our job to walk it out. If we know we are, we know we are pleasing to God, no matter how it feels. God evaluates justly, and He always decides in our favor.

There is therefore now no condemnation to them which are in Christ Jesus, who walk not after the flesh, but after the Spirit.

– Romans 8:1

20. Sufficient unto the day are the requirements thereof, and God's grace is sufficient for you for those requirements

And he said unto me, My grace is sufficient for thee: for my strength is made perfect in weakness. Most gladly therefore will I rather glory in my infirmities, that the power of Christ may rest upon me.

–2 Corinthians 12: 9

21. The key to mastery is alone time, to grapple with the complexities of any art, science, skill, or knowledge base, whether it be the mastery of the violin or piano, understanding the complexities of stock trading, or the research and discovery of a cure or invention.

Through desire a man, having separated himself, seeketh and intermeddleth with all wisdom.

– Proverbs 18:1

22. Only you can decide to dedicate to the discipline of increasing in knowledge, wisdom, and skill. No one else can determine your habits. And no one else can determine your rewards.

He that getteth wisdom loveth his own soul:
he that keepeth understanding shall find good.

– Proverbs 19:8

23. There is a system that uses fear to create imaginary barriers for new entrants into the competition for a successful

life. However, those who courageously run through the troops and jump over that wall will soon discover a fruitful valley that they are well able to possess!

And Caleb stilled the people before Moses, and said, Let us go up at once, and possess it; for we are well able to overcome it.

— Numbers 13:30

24. If you stay where life is moving, you will move with life!

For to him that is joined to all the living there is hope: for a living dog is better than a dead lion.

— Ecclesiastes 9:4

25. If God is working in any area of your life, God is working in every area of your life. When your life is in God's hands, He leaves no area untouched.

And we know that all things work together for good to them that love God, to them who are the called according to his purpose.

— Romans 8:28

26. In regards to our past, we must properly discern between buried treasure and dried bones. Treasures increase in value over time. Dry bones are useless and should stay in their grave. There are certain people, places, and events of our past that can enrich our future. However, useless artifacts can only haunt the beautiful new beginnings God wants to give us.

He that walketh with wise men shall be wise: but a companion of fools shall be destroyed.

– Proverbs 13:20

27. Don't be controlled or navigated by someone whose morals, purity of heart, level of excellence, or spiritual compass is less than your own, no matter what their level of greatness, experience, or accomplishment. They can only lead you according to their own level of pureness of heart. Learn what you can, but make your own final decisions.

A good man out of the good treasure of his heart bringeth forth that which is good; and an evil man out of the evil treasure of his heart bringeth forth that which is evil: for of the abundance of the heart his mouth speaketh.

– Luke 6:45

28. As the refining of silver and gold increases its beauty, value, attractiveness, and worth through the application of heat, so is a man or woman increased in value, beauty, profitability, potential, and worth through reading, study, practice and discipline.

As the fining pot for silver, and the furnace for gold; so is a man to his praise.

– Proverbs 27:21

29. Do not initiate behavior that is not sustainable or that promises no enduring reward.

Distinguished Wisdom Presents . . . "Living Proverbs"-Vol.1

He that tilleth his land shall have plenty of bread: but he that followeth after vain persons shall have poverty enough.

— Proverbs 28:19

30. Some people just want to be right. Some people just don't want to be wrong. There is a vast difference between the two. A teachable spirit, or the lack thereof, makes the difference.

Reprove not a scorner, lest he hate thee:
rebuke a wise man, and he will love thee.

— Proverbs 9:8

31. If you have a larger vision than the vision of the house you came out of, support your vision.

To do justice and judgment is more acceptable to the Lord than sacrifice.

— Proverbs 21:3

32. God prefers progress instead of pacifiers.

Therefore leaving the principles of the doctrine of Christ, let us go on unto perfection; not laying again the foundation of repentance from dead works, and of faith toward God.

— Hebrews 6:1

33. Release the day ceremony:

Say, "I did my best today. God accepts that. I accept that."

Have a peaceful nights rest.

–From your heavenly Father

It is vain for you to rise up early, to sit up late, to eat the bread of sorrows: for so he giveth his beloved sleep.

– Psalms 126:2

34. Live daily before an audience of one, and daily you will bless many. Only God knows the true intentions of your heart, whether good or bad. If we seek to please Him, by His grace, we will always be successful in His sight. God, our heavenly Father, always decides in our favor. He always believes the best of us. He is always there to give us the grace we need in order to fulfill our responsibility to Him. In doing so, we will fulfill our responsibility to others. And that's all that can truly be asked for.

For the word of God is quick, and powerful, and sharper than any twoedged sword, piercing even to the dividing asunder of soul and spirit, and of the joints and marrow, and is a discerner of the thoughts and intents of the heart. Neither is there any creature that is not manifest in his sight: but all things are naked and opened unto the eyes of him with whom we have to do.

– Hebrews 4:12–13

35. If you want tomorrow, you have to fight for it today!

So teach us to number our days,
that we may apply our hearts unto wisdom.

– Psalm 90:12

36. God can trust you to organize your own time and seek your own provision. You don't need a boss, supervisor, or alarm clock to make you get up and be productive because you know winter is coming, and you've got to eat!

Go to the ant, thou sluggard;
consider her ways, and be wise:
which having no guide, overseer, or ruler,
provideth her meat in the summer,
and gathereth her food in the harvest.

– Proverbs 6:6–8

37. God loves everyone. He so loved the world that He gave Jesus to die on the cross to pay for all of our sins and raised Him from the dead for our salvation. However, God our Father has a special love and affection for the people that seek Him sincerely. Those who seek God's principles for living, with the intent to obey, will receive the benefits that come with salvation. Sincere love for God, through diligent obedience to His principles, brings the promised benefits of salvation.

I love them that love me;
and those that seek me early shall find me.
Riches and honour are with me;
yea, durable riches and righteousness.
My fruit is better than gold, yea, than fine gold;
and my revenue than choice silver.
I lead in the way of righteousness,
in the midst of the paths of judgment:
that I may cause those that love me to inherit substance; and I will fill their treasures.

– Proverbs 8:17–21

38. I declare God's notable favor upon you and yours. In Jesus name, amen.

And thus shall ye say to him that liveth in prosperity, Peace be both to thee, and peace be to thine house, and peace be unto all that thou hast.

–1 Samuel 25:6

39. Plan for tomorrow, but master today. Today's journey is your chief responsibility. Today's success creates the path for tomorrow's success and fulfillment.

Boast not thyself of to morrow;
for thou knowest not what a day may bring forth.

– Proverbs 27:1

40. The degree of information that you gather on any subject of study will determine the eventual degree of formation that subject takes in your mind. You will then eventually see the big picture!

Wisdom is the principal thing; therefore get wisdom: and with all thy getting get understanding.

– Proverbs 4:7

41. A man of diplomacy has many friends. A man of truth has true friends.

He that rebuketh a man afterwards shall find more favour than he that flattereth with the tongue.

– Proverbs 28:23

42. Surround yourself with people that believe!

Simon Peter, a servant and an apostle of Jesus Christ, to them that have obtained like precious faith with us through the righteousness of God and our Saviour Jesus Christ:

–2 Peter 1:1

43. Enjoy today. Believe God for tomorrow.

Take therefore no thought for the morrow: for the morrow shall take thought for the things of itself. Sufficient unto the day is the evil thereof.

– Matthew 6:34

44. Just like the eagle takes time daily to preen its feathers to maintain its ability to soar, we must take time to restore ourselves daily through spending time with God in the Word and prayer.

Now ye are clean through the word which I have spoken unto you.

– John 15:3

45. In regard to career, occupation, gifting and calling the indication of what you are is evidenced and measured by the kind of fruit you bear. Just like you have evidence of an apple, pear, or orange tree by the kind of fruit it bears, identity is not determined by the money associated with the tree; it's evidenced by the fruit it bears. As we focus on bearing the fruit, which is native to the type of tree we are, the money will follow, based on the marketing of that fruit in the marketplace.

Ye shall know them by their fruits. Do men gather grapes of thorns, or figs of thistles? Even so every good tree bringeth forth good fruit; but a corrupt tree bringeth forth evil fruit. A good tree cannot bring forth evil fruit, neither can a corrupt tree bring forth good fruit. Every tree that bringeth not forth good fruit is hewn down, and cast into the fire. Wherefore by their fruits ye shall know them.

– Matthew 7:16–20

46. A good idea, or rather a "God idea," is a seed planted by God into your spirit. It becomes your responsibility. A concept is the seed of an idea developed into an embryo. We must properly protect it and nourish it in order to finally birth a product, service, or solution worth having. We must continue to invest in it and attend to it in order for it to reach the intended destiny for which the seed was sown in the beginning. The reward will always be wealth, happiness, peace, and satisfaction. However, to obtain the reward, it always requires diligent commitment.

The slothful man roasteth not that which he took in hunting: but the substance of a diligent man is precious.

– Proverbs 12:27

47. Leadership is a constant exercise of making decisions in the face of ambiguity. Ambiguity means doubtfulness or uncertainty of meaning, unclear or indefinite. However, God promises to lead those who seek Him. Following His lead is a sign of maturity.

For as many as are led by the Spirit of God, they are the sons of God.

– Romans 8:14

48. True love gives wings, not strings.

Now the Lord is that Spirit: and where the Spirit of the Lord is, there is liberty.

−2 Corinthians 3:17

49. Early is an advantage. On time is average. Late is unacceptable.

Seest thou a man diligent in his business? he shall stand before kings; he shall not stand before mean men.

− Proverbs 22:29

(Statistically, the *mean* is the *average*.)

50. Riches is money with wings. Wealth is riches with roots.

Wilt thou set thine eyes upon that which is not? for riches certainly make themselves wings; they fly away as an eagle toward heaven.

− Proverbs 23:5

51. First impressions are lasting impressions. Last impressions are lasting impressions. Every impression is a first impression and a last impression.

Mark the perfect man, and behold the upright: for the end of that man is peace.

− Psalm 37:37

52. There's a difference between being focused and being narrow. Focus is necessary for success. Narrowness limits your perspective, and thus, it limits success.

And God gave Solomon wisdom and understanding exceeding much, and largeness of heart, even as the sand that is on the sea shore.

– 1 Kings 4:29

53. You are not where you are. You are who you are. And who you are will determine where you will finish up.

Before I formed you in the belly I knew you: and before you came forth out of the womb I sanctified you, and I ordained you a prophet unto the nations.

– Jeremiah 1:5

54. Just like an expert surfer, we have to learn how to ride every wave of blessing as far we can take it, always looking and expecting the next big wave. Don't be so quick to wipe out after each wave of blessing. Keep on rejoicing! Keep on praising! Keep on singing! Keep on being thankful! The next big wave is coming soon!

Blessed be the Lord, who daily loadeth us with benefits, even the God of our salvation. Selah.

– Psalm 68:19

55. You have been walking on the water this far; there is no need to get nervous now. Just keep on stepping out on the Word of Jesus. He told you to "Come." You will make it to the

other side. You will make it to your promised, expected place of blessing!

And Peter answered him and said, Lord, if it be thou, bid me come unto thee on the water. And he said, Come. And when Peter was come down out of the ship, he walked on the water, to go to Jesus. But when he saw the wind boisterous, he was afraid; and beginning to sink, he cried, saying, Lord, save me. And immediately Jesus stretched forth his hand, and caught him, and said unto him, O thou of little faith, wherefore didst thou doubt?

– Matthew 14:28–31

56. Sage marriage counsel:

A bird in the hand is better than two in the bush

The grass may look greener on the other side, but it probably has a snake hiding in the grass. It has weeds and thorns.

Better is the sight of the eyes than the wandering of the desire: this is also vanity and vexation of spirit.

– Ecclesiastes 6:9

57. Where there's a willing will, there's a witty way!

Now therefore perform the doing of it; that as there was a readiness to will, so there may be a performance also out of that which ye have. For if there be first a willing mind, it is accepted according to that a man hath, and not according to that he hath not.

–2 Corinthians 8:11–12

58. If you can think of it, it can be done. No matter what your highest thought, dream, or aspiration may be, God can top it. If we will fill our heart with faith, through reading, meditating upon, and hearing God's Word, nothing shall be impossible to us.

Ephesians 3:20 says, "Now unto him that is able to do exceeding abundantly above all that we ask or think, according to the power that worketh in us." The only thing that stands in the way of the righteous doing great exploits is fear. However, Proverbs 28:1 says, "The wicked fleeth when no man pursueth: but the righteous are *bold as a lion*!" Luke 1:36 says, "For with God nothing shall be impossible!"

Jesus said in Matthew 17:20–21, "And Jesus said unto them, Because of your unbelief: for verily I say unto you, If ye have faith as a grain of mustard seed, ye shall say unto this mountain, Remove hence to yonder place; and it shall remove; and nothing shall be impossible unto you. 21 Howbeit this kind goeth not out but by prayer and fasting." So we see nothing is impossible if we provide the preparation and the action of faith!

59. Excellence requires the time that it takes. Never cut corners. Never allow the pressure of others to make you violate your own internal standard of excellence. People pay for the best. People don't pay for mess. This is applicable in business, on the job, or in relationships. Always present your best as a representation of your internal standard of excellence. This is all people have to judge you by in the final analysis. Excellence requires no explanation.

Whatsoever thy hand findeth to do, do it with thy might; for there is no work, nor device, nor knowledge, nor wisdom, in the grave, whither thou goest.

– Ecclesiastes 9:10

60. Know thyself, and to thine own self be true. Recognize your own value, and spend time refining it. Work on yourself and that which only you can produce. This is the key to happiness and true success. This is each person's divine responsibility.

Wherefore I perceive that there is nothing better, than that a man should rejoice in his own works; for that is his portion: for who shall bring him to see what shall be after him?

– Ecclesiastes 3:22

61. Let your forty years of war on your job, in business, and in life create forty years of peace for your children and your children's children, just like King David spent forty years of his life establishing the kingdom of Israel for God. His forty years of warfare created the ability for his son King Solomon to reign in forty years of peace. "A good man leaves an inheritance for his children's children." (Proverbs 13:22) The limited view of a father providing for his family is forty hours a week for forty years, with the anticipation of leaving a pension, a social security check, and a life insurance policy. However, God's view is for that same man to discover the gifts and talents God gave him and build a financial legacy or organization to leave to his children's children. Provision can be thought of in the short view or it can be worked on from

the long view. It will take the same amount of years— there's just a different focus and perspective.

A good man leaveth an inheritance to his children's children: and the wealth of the sinner is laid up for the just.

– Proverbs 13:22

62. Make your private pursuit of preparation a priority in order for you to be a public benefit.

The preparations of the heart in man, and the answer of the tongue, is from the Lord.

– Proverbs 16:1

63. We should live our lives by three bands:

1. Band the belly.
2. Band the wallet.
3. Band the wrist.

Band the belly by monitoring how much we eat. Band the wallet by monitoring how much we spend. Band the wrist by wearing a watch and monitoring our time and time management. We should live our lives by three bands.

When thou sittest to eat with a ruler,
consider diligently what is before thee:
and put a knife to thy throat,
if thou be a man given to appetite.

– Proverbs 23:1–2

Be thou diligent to know the state of thy flocks,
and look well to thy herds. For riches are not for ever: and doth the crown endure to every generation?

– Proverbs 27:23–24

So teach us to number our days,
that we may apply our hearts unto wisdom.

– Psalm 90:12

64. No matter what your trouble may be, and no matter how difficult it may seem, when you're in trouble, you become God's top priority. The LORD will not leave or forsake the righteous in trouble. You are His primary priority.

But the salvation of the righteous is of the Lord: he is their strength in the time of trouble.

– Psalm 37:39

65. Do not be safe; be successful!

I returned, and saw under the sun, that the race is not to the swift, nor the battle to the strong, neither yet bread to the wise, nor yet riches to men of understanding, nor yet favour to men of skill; but time and chance happeneth to them all.

– Ecclesiastes 9:11

66. No matter what trouble may be in the earth, and no matter who thinks he or she is in power, our GOD *reigns!* Jehovah God is the Most High God! Every man's power is held on a string— fragile and fleeting. No one has the power to

truly uphold him or herself. Only God is truly in control. Our GOD reigns!

Now I Nebuchadnezzar praise and extol and honour the King of heaven, all whose works are truth, and his ways judgment: and those that walk in pride he is able to abase.

– Daniel 4:37

67. This is not the end. God has a plan for long–term, lifelong provision and a good sustained future. He's smarter than all of us, you know? And He never does anything half way. He started it, and He will finish it in grand style! You can depend on Him. Believe Him above your circumstances. Your faith helps to strengthen you and release His power. However, His plan for you was set from the beginning. He always succeeds with His plan. We cooperate with our faith, worship, prayer, and living right and doing the right thing. God loves you. He will never fail you!

Being confident of this very thing, that he which hath begun a good work in you will perform it until the day of Jesus Christ.

– Philippians 1:6

68. There's no hopeless situation to the person with a promise. You have the promises of God.

Whereby are given unto us exceeding great and precious promises: that by these ye might be partakers of the divine nature, having escaped the corruption that is in the world through lust.

–2 Peter 1:4

69. The world's not going down on our watch! If you agree, say amen!

If my people, which are called by my name, shall humble themselves, and pray, and seek my face, and turn from their wicked ways; then will I hear from heaven, and will forgive their sin, and will heal their land.

–2 Chronicles 7:14

70. The key to following God is to shift your life into forward motion; continue to take steps, always seeking God. Be ready to shift to the right or left or yield and be still. Be ever postured for forward motion, but always listening for current, updated instructions. Living prayerfully and obediently is the key.

Seek the Lord and his strength,
seek his face continually.

–1 Chronicles 16:11

71. It takes faith to believe and release the power of God. It takes trust to believe and receive from the faithfulness of God.

Let us hold fast the profession of our faith without wavering; (for he is faithful that promised;)

– Hebrews 10:23

72. Truly great people are gracious people.

That thou mayest walk in the way of good men, and keep the paths of the righteous.

– Proverbs 2:20

73. The foundation of a stable, sustainable life is the fear and reverence of the living, holy God; Jehovah is His name! He is the Ancient of Days, from which all wisdom, knowledge, and understanding flows. He is the Creator and Genesis of all things. Once we gain a proper, healthy reverence of God in all things, we can then build upon all other available knowledge for the progress and advancement of our lives. We should live from the foundation of our healthy reverence and relationship with Him. That relationship is established by accepting His Way and reconciler back to Himself: the Lord Jesus Christ.

The fear of the Lord is the beginning of knowledge: but fools despise wisdom and instruction.

– Proverbs 1:7

74. Sometimes life might seem like a maze, but God is amazing! Trust in the Lord. He has a clear plan.

Trust in the Lord with all thine heart;
and lean not unto thine own understanding.
In all thy ways acknowledge him,
and he shall direct thy paths.

– Proverbs 3:5–6

75. If you feel like you are becoming weak in the race, or you are becoming tired in the struggle— if you feel like you are barely hanging on for dear life— then please tie a knot in

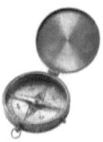

the rope of hope and hang on! God is faithful. I know He will strengthen you for your journey. You may not know how, but if you will remain faithful in doing the right things, you will see God bring you out. He will change your night into a brighter, fuller day! You will be stronger in the end.

The righteous also shall hold on his way, and he that hath clean hands shall be stronger and stronger.

– Job 17:9

76. Those who go the extra mile will go the extra mile; and the extra mile wins the race. Most worthwhile races in life are distance races and not sprints. The wise fight to finish in order to gain the prize.

Thus Solomon finished the house of The Lord, and the king's house: and all that came into Solomon's heart to make in the house of The Lord, and in his own house, he prosperously effected.

–2 Chronicles 7:11

77. Good customs make good remedies work for you. When you have a lifestyle that practices good, godly customs or habits and you are faced with an occasional unusual ordeal or challenge, you will be able to quickly take some prescribed remedy to come out of it quickly. Your regular good customs will make the needed remedy work quickly and effectively for you.

It is like a person who has a lifestyle of good rest, good healthy eating habits, drinking plenty of water, eating plenty of fruits and vegetables, and regular exercise. If this person catches the occasional cold or flu symptom, he or she will be

able to shake it quickly with the doctors prescribed remedy of a quick course of antibiotics. He or she may also add some extra old fashioned home remedies like lemon and honey tea, etc. All in all, this person will be able to shake the symptoms quickly because she or he has a healthy lifestyle.

However, if those same symptoms hit a person with an unhealthy lifestyle of smoking, drugs, alcohol, lack of proper rest, and/or a diet full of salty, fatty, fried foods, and little or no fruits and vegetables and water, this person will have a more difficult time of having simple remedies relieve them of the same symptoms.

Jesus maintained good customs that allowed Him to be effective on the earth during His ministry. Jesus maintained a lifestyle of prayer, reading the Word, and going to church. This prepared Him to perform His ministry. We also should maintain the same customs. Good customs make good remedies work for you.

And he came to Nazareth, where he had been brought up: and, as his custom was, he went into the synagogue on the sabbath day, and stood up for to read. And there was delivered unto him the book of the prophet Esaias. And when he had opened the book, he found the place where it was written, The Spirit of the Lord is upon me, because he hath anointed me to preach the gospel to the poor; he hath sent me to heal the brokenhearted, to preach deliverance to the captives, and recovering of sight to the blind, to set at liberty them that are bruised, to preach the acceptable year of the Lord. And he closed the book, and he gave it again to the minister, and sat down.

– Luke 4:16–20

78. A laser focused can cut through steel!

Through desire a man, having separated himself, seeketh and intermeddleth with all wisdom.

– Proverbs 18:1

78. If it seems as if life has gotten wild and thrown you out of the saddle, please, jump back up, dust yourself off, and jump back on the horse! Your destiny is still promised. Fight for your dream, and ride it all the way in!

The steps of a good man are ordered by the Lord: and he delighteth in his way. Though he fall, he shall not be utterly cast down: for the Lord upholdeth him with his hand.

– Psalm 37:23–24

80. Envision the future you desire for tomorrow while it is still called today. Then, throw your lasso of faith forward into tomorrow and grab hold of your more desirable future and draw it, pull it, reel it into your today. Your daily, tenacious habits of faith is your power to change your today into a brighter, more prosperous tomorrow!

Now faith is the substance of things hoped for, the evidence of things not seen. For by it the elders obtained a good report. Through faith we understand that the worlds were framed by the word of God, so that things which are seen were not made of things which do appear.

– Hebrews 11:1–3

81. Realized dreams are not only written on perishable paper in temporary ink; they are etched in the stones of time by the pen of effort.

And the Lord answered me, and said,
Write the vision, and make it plain upon tables, that he may run that readeth it.
For the vision is yet for an appointed time,
but at the end it shall speak, and not lie:
though it tarry, wait for it; because it will surely come, it will not tarry.
Behold, his soul which is lifted up is not upright in him: but the just shall live by his faith.

– Habakkuk 2:2–4

82. We are the just. We walk by faith and not by feelings because sometimes feelings are not appealing. The joy of the Lord is our strength. We can choose to praise the Lord. We can choose to stay positive. We have the strength to choose.

For we walk by faith, not by sight.

−2 Corinthians 5:7

83. Run the race to win! Walk by faith and not by sight! Having done all to stand— stand!

Know ye not that they which run in a race run all, but one receiveth the prize? So run, that ye may obtain.

−1 Corinthians 9:24

For we walk by faith, not by sight.

−2 Corinthians 5:7

Wherefore take unto you the whole armour of God, that ye may be able to withstand in the evil day, and having done all, to stand.

– Ephesians 6:13

84. We should spend our time, energy, and expertise in such a way that we leave something tangible to the next generation. We've all been taught to work hard daily, yet many haven't been taught how to invest their daily supply of life in such a way that they have something left over for their children's children. The long view should be the daily focus.

A good man leaveth an inheritance to his children's children: and the wealth of the sinner is laid up for the just. Much food is in the tillage of the poor: but there is that is destroyed for want of judgment.

– Proverbs 13:22–23

85. It takes self-control to curb the release of an angry tongue's retaliation to a perceived offense. However, for peace's sake, some things are better left unsaid.

A soft answer turneth away wrath:
but grievous words stir up anger.

– Proverbs 15:1

86. God has great plans for your life. This is the best and most exciting time to be alive. You were born for such a time as this. God has a great plan for you, your children, and your grandchildren. Live holy and right, like He could come tomorrow, but plan and live with positive expectations and make preparations for future generations.

For I know the thoughts that I think toward you, saith the Lord, thoughts of peace, and not of evil, to give you an expected end.

– Jeremiah 29:11

87. Let us all pray for all people of our nation and the nations of the world. The pain of one person in any nation is the pain of all people in every nation. God is able to cure all people and deliver all through the blood of Jesus Christ.

For God so loved the world, that he gave his only begotten Son, that whosoever believeth in him should not perish, but have everlasting life. For God sent not his Son into the world to condemn the world; but that the world through him might be saved.

– John 3:16–17

88. God's Word is not about religion for religion's sake. Obeying God's Word is about doing what's right for life. If we all would live by His Word, we could solve all societal problems. If we obey His natural laws, we could access His supernatural power.

Thus speaketh the Lord of hosts, saying, Execute true judgment, and shew mercy and compassions every man to his brother: and oppress not the widow, nor the fatherless, the stranger, nor the poor; and let none of you imagine evil against his brother in your heart.

– Zechariah 7:9–10

89. Let us not be anxious or afraid for our future, for God has His hand on the reins of life. He controls the bands of balance, and He knows how to draw back the forces of darkness. We have power in the earth to bind the Devil and release the power of God to work on our behalf. Prayer is the key.

Rejoice in the Lord alway: and again I say, Rejoice. Let your moderation be known unto all men. The Lord is at hand. Be careful for nothing; but in every thing by prayer and supplication with thanksgiving let your requests be made known unto God. And the peace of God, which passeth all understanding, shall keep your hearts and minds through Christ Jesus. Finally, brethren, whatsoever things are true, whatsoever things are honest, whatsoever things are just, whatsoever things are pure, whatsoever things are lovely, whatsoever things are of good report; if there be any virtue, and if there be any praise, think on these things. Those things, which ye have both learned, and received, and heard, and seen in me, do: and the God of peace shall be with you.

– Philippians 4:4–9

90. The difference between a dreamer and a fool is continual right action!

For a dream cometh through the multitude of business; and a fool's voice is known by multitude of words.

– Ecclesiastes 5:3

91. Faith is our first and final course of action. Everything else is supplemental. Medicine, vitamins and herbal remedies, etc., all have their place. However, the just "shall" live by faith.

So then faith cometh by hearing, and hearing by the word of God.

– Romans 10:17

92. What do you call a talking horse?

A neigh-sayer

A merry heart maketh a cheerful countenance:
but by sorrow of the heart the spirit is broken.

– Proverbs 15:13

93. Some of us are getting ready to surprise the world! Through discovery of the gifts and talents given by almighty God, and through diligence and discipline, we are about to come forth to the foreground of life. God enjoys making the last, first. He enjoys taking those that have been in the background, working on their gifts in secret, and presenting them on center stage. All to the glory of God!

But God hath chosen the foolish things of the world to confound the wise; and God hath chosen the weak things of the world to confound the things which are mighty; and base things of the world, and things which are despised, hath God chosen, yea, and things which are not, to bring to nought things that are: that no flesh should glory in his presence. But of him are ye in Christ Jesus, who of God is made unto us wisdom, and righteousness, and sanctification, and redemption: that, according as it is written, He that glorieth, let him glory in the Lord.

–1 Corinthians 1:27–31

94. We will only be rewarded for what we actually do. We can study about it and we can listen to preaching about it, but we will only be paid for what we actually do. The better and sooner we do it usually will determine the more and sooner we are rewarded for it.

But whoso looketh into the perfect law of liberty, and continueth therein, he being not a forgetful hearer, but a doer of the work, this man shall be blessed in his deed.

– James 1:25

95. Read, listen to, meditate, obey, and stick with the Word and you will ultimately gain the blessing for which the Lord sent the Word. Wisdom is the principle thing; therefore, study, listen to, and meditate the Word with the purpose of gaining understanding.

But whoso looketh into the perfect law of liberty, and continueth therein, he being not a forgetful hearer, but a doer of the work, this man shall be blessed in his deed.

–James 1:25

96. Skill is the key to distinction in any job, occupation, or endeavor.

Seest thou a man diligent in his business? he shall stand before kings; he shall not stand before mean men.

– Proverbs 22:29

97. Marriage advice to husbands:

Lead.
Take charge.
Take responsibility.

—Bishop T.D. Jakes

For the husband is the head of the wife, even as Christ is the head of the church: and he is the savior of the body. Therefore as the church is subject unto Christ, so let the wives be to their own husbands in

everything. Husbands, love your wives, even as Christ also loved the church, and gave himself for it;

– Ephesians 5:23–25

98. Take time today and read several chapters of the Bible. Get on a regular Bible reading schedule. It will benefit your life and give order and godly counsel to your every daily decision.

The law of the Lord is perfect, converting the soul: the testimony of the Lord is sure, making wise the simple. The statutes of the Lord are right, rejoicing the heart: the commandment of the Lord is pure, enlightening the eyes. The fear of the Lord is clean, enduring for ever:
the judgments of the Lord are true and righteous altogether. More to be desired are they than gold, yea, than much fine gold:
sweeter also than honey and the honeycomb.
Moreover by them is thy servant warned:
and in keeping of them there is great reward.

– Psalm 19:7–11

99. Value wisdom enough to invest in it. Buy books and audio and video success teaching series, and attend workshops and seminars on the subjects that are aligned with your core gifts, talents, and purpose. Invest your time and money into what really matters. Invest in what's going to payoff within a certain amount of time.

Buy the truth, and sell it not; also wisdom, and instruction, and understanding.

– Proverbs 23:23

100. Continue to walk by faith, guided by the written Word of God and His principles, even when you do not have the luxury of feelings to confirm the validity of your every move. We are the just. We "walk by faith and not by sight." (2 Corinthians 5:7)

For we walk by faith, not by sight.

-2 Corinthians 5:7

101. Do you still believe? Just a little bit?

If so, that's all the faith you need to change the world! You can still obtain your miracle in life. You can still obtain your dream. Jesus said all you need is "faith like a mustard seed." (Matthew 17:20) All that matters is that you plant your faith through your words and actions. Your dream can still blossom into a mighty tree of reality in your life!

Now faith is the substance of things hoped for, the evidence of things not seen. For by it the elders obtained a good report. Through faith we understand that the worlds were framed by the word of God, so that things which are seen were not made of things which do appear.

– Hebrews 11:1-3

102. Do not be moved by the current circumstances of your life and those in the world. There has always been conflict, struggle, sickness, joy, healing, and redemption in the world since the history of man's story began. God knows how to preserve His people until the final day of redemption!

To every thing there is a season,
and a time to every purpose under the heaven:
a time to be born, and a time to die;
a time to plant, and a time to pluck up that which is planted;
a time to kill, and a time to heal;
a time to break down, and a time to build up;
a time to weep, and a time to laugh;
a time to mourn, and a time to dance;
a time to cast away stones,
and a time to gather stones together;
a time to embrace, and a time to refrain from embracing;
a time to get, and a time to lose;
a time to keep, and a time to cast away;
a time to rend, and a time to sew;
a time to keep silence, and a time to speak;
a time to love, and a time to hate;
a time of war, and a time of peace.

– Ecclesiastes 3:1–8

103. Write it. Speak it. See it. Do it!

And the Lord answered me, and said,
Write the vision, and make it plain upon tables, that he may run that readeth it.
For the vision is yet for an appointed time,
but at the end it shall speak, and not lie:
though it tarry, wait for it; because it will surely come, it will not tarry.
Behold, his soul which is lifted up is not upright in him: but the just shall live by his faith.

– Habakkuk 2:2–4

104. When you know you're right, you have no reason to be fearful. You can go into a situation or circumstance and make a demand boldly for what you know you have a right to. There is no shame, no intimidation, and no insecurity to a righteous, upright person.

The wicked flee when no man pursueth:
but the righteous are bold as a lion.

– Proverbs 28:1

105. Qualified leadership by righteous men and women is the key to American prosperity and preservation. We must seek to become qualified and involved and take the lead to save the nation.

When the righteous are in authority, the people rejoice: but when the wicked beareth rule, the people mourn.

– Proverbs 29:2

106. Dreams that stay in the womb will go to the tomb. Dreams that are birthed will have eventual worth.

For a dream cometh through the multitude of business; and a fool's voice is known by multitude of words.

– Ecclesiastes 5:3

107. Your life's story will be written in the opportunities you took and the opportunities you failed to take.

Whatsoever thy hand findeth to do, do it with thy might; for there is no work, nor device, nor knowledge, nor wisdom, in the grave,

whither thou goest. I returned, and saw under the sun, that the race is not to the swift, nor the battle to the strong, neither yet bread to the wise, nor yet riches to men of understanding, nor yet favour to men of skill; but time and chance happeneth to them all.

– Ecclesiastes 9:10–11

108. Those who are led by their spirit are led by the Spirit faster than their minds can conceive. When you're led by God's schedule and plan, you are often led by your spirit faster than your mind can conceive. You just travel according to God's scheduling. The renewed mind eventually catches up and realizes that you were actually being led by the Spirit. Because you have a mature, submissive, alert, and available spirit, God can lead you by His Spirit faster than your mind can conceive.

For as many as are led by the Spirit of God, they are the sons of God.

– Romans 8:14

109. The difference from being a wage earner to becoming a wealth builder is to convert from being paid by the hour to being paid by the product. It's true whether you're making and selling cars, cell phones, watches, or match sticks!

Every man also to whom God hath given riches and wealth, and hath given him power to eat thereof, and to take his portion, and to rejoice in his labour; this is the gift of God.

– Ecclesiastes 5:19

110. If your past is unnecessary to reach the future you envision, detach from your past, and pursue the vision of your future.

And the manna ceased on the morrow after they had eaten of the old corn of the land; neither had the children of Israel manna any more; but they did eat of the fruit of the land of Canaan that year.

– Joshua 5:12

111. The person who treads alongside the path of a wise champion will eventually develop a similar manner of marching through life. He or she will pick up the mannerisms, habits, and wisdom of the champion, becoming wise him or herself. This can be done through the study of books or in personal interaction. Choose your champions wisely!

He that walketh with wise men shall be wise:
but a companion of fools shall be destroyed.

– Proverbs 13:20

112. You were made in the image and likeness of God Himself. You were made to have full authority over the earth in your sphere of influence, gifting, and responsibility. God Himself pays close attention to your request in prayer. You are empowered. In Jesus name, amen!

What is man, that thou art mindful of him?
and the son of man, that thou visitest him?
For thou hast made him a little lower than the angels, and hast crowned him with glory and honour. Thou madest him to have dominion over the works of thy hands; thou hast put all things under his feet: all sheep and oxen, yea, and the beasts of the field;

the fowl of the air, and the fish of the sea, and whatsoever passeth through the paths of the seas. O Lord our Lord, how excellent is thy name in all the earth!

– Psalm 8:4–9

113. The Bible is the living Word of God. It is the source of life and guidance for our daily living. Start the day by reading it. It will guide your day.

Hear, O my son, and receive my sayings;
and the years of thy life shall be many.
I have taught thee in the way of wisdom;
I have led thee in right paths. When thou goest, thy steps shall not be straitened; and when thou runnest, thou shalt not stumble. Take fast hold of instruction; let her not go: keep her; for she is thy life.

– Proverbs 4:10–13

114. You are well able to fulfill your every responsibility. You are empowered to prosper and succeed in life. His strength is made perfect in your weakness. You can be eternally strong inwardly, even when you feel weak outwardly. Your boost of strength is one prayer away.

I can do all things through Christ which strengtheneth me.

– Philippians 4:13

115. The purpose of our work is for us to enjoy ourselves in our work and to be able to enjoy good in life and to do good. Work is a means of disciplining the soul and focusing the mind so we can get the greatest benefit out of life and in the end be thankful only to God for His precious gift.

What profit hath he that worketh in that wherein he laboureth? I have seen the travail, which God hath given to the sons of men to be exercised in it. He hath made every thing beautiful in his time: also he hath set the world in their heart, so that no man can find out the work that God maketh from the beginning to the end. I know that there is no good in them, but for a man to rejoice, and to do good in his life. And also that every man should eat and drink, and enjoy the good of all his labour, it is the gift of God.

– Ecclesiastes 3:9–13

116. Ultimately, we are all dependent on God. Flesh is like grass, and the beauty thereof is as the flower of the grass. We all must trust in the Lord for our daily bread, protection, and health. The Lord is our Shepherd; we shall not want.

My soul, wait thou only upon God;
for my expectation is from him.
He only is my rock and my salvation:
he is my defence; I shall not be moved

– Psalm 62:5–6

117. No matter what your test, trial, challenge, or tragedy may be at this moment, God is your source of strength, confidence, and refuge. He will uphold you for every situation.

In the fear of the Lord is strong confidence: and his children shall have a place of refuge.

– Proverbs 14:26

118. Wise is the person who asks God for help and willingly gives Him thanksgiving, glory, and service in exchange.

Thus saith the Lord,
Let not the wise man glory in his wisdom,
neither let the mighty man glory in his might,
let not the rich man glory in his riches:
but let him that glorieth glory in this,
that he understandeth and knoweth me,
that I am the Lord which exercise lovingkindness, judgment, and righteousness, in the earth: for in these things I delight, saith the Lord.

– Jeremiah 9:23–24

119. The thing about favor is that you don't really have to earn it. However, you can increase your occurrences of favor and reward, through diligent pursuits of right and good, and through practicing excellence in your pursuits.

He that diligently seeketh good procureth favour: but he that seeketh mischief, it shall come unto him.

– Proverbs 11:27

120. The step of faith that you take today will determine your capacity for God's abundance tomorrow. The just shall live by faith. Keep taking steps of faith. This will determine what kind of future you will obtain. Those who plan to live by stretching and taking continual steps of faith increase their propensity toward a longer, more fulfilling future and life.

The steps of a good man are ordered by the Lord: and he delighteth in his way.

– Psalm 37:23

121. Dig deep. Mine your gold. Do not take it to the grave. The graveyard is too rich. Your life is your opportunity to enrich the earth. Leave your treasure on this side. You will receive your reward on that side!

Whatsoever thy hand findeth to do, do it with thy might; for there is no work, nor device, nor knowledge, nor wisdom, in the grave, whither thou goest

– Ecclesiastes 9:10

122. The Lord will always put certain people in your life along the way to help you. Be thankful for them, always putting your ultimate trust in the Lord.

It is better to trust in the Lord than to put confidence in man. It is better to trust in the Lord than to put confidence in princes.

– Psalm 118:8–9

123. The key to financial wealth, prosperity, happiness, and social freedom is to develop the habit of unearthing and cultivating the God-given treasure within you. The key to endless poverty is wasting time on fruitless pursuits, people, and places.

He that tilleth his land shall be satisfied with bread: but he that followeth vain persons is void of understanding.

– Proverbs 12:11

124. One of the keys to become the person God created you to be is the associations you have. Through meditating God's Word, reading good books, and associating with prosperous people, you too will become prosperous and wise.

He that walketh with wise men shall be wise: but a companion of fools shall be destroyed.

– Proverbs 13:20

125. God has big plans for you! Live with high expectation! Plan for the future. And don't sabotage your tomorrow by making bad choices today!

For I know the thoughts that I think toward you, saith the Lord, thoughts of peace, and not of evil, to give you an expected end.

– Jeremiah 29:11

126. Diligent, persistent, effort releases your inheritance. "Now faith" means to take action today for what you believe you receive today. Everything takes steps. Today's action steps ensure the blessing you have received by faith today. God can and will put His wind behind your back, but it still requires a certain amount of natural time, preparation, and action steps to achieve great goals.

A man shall be satisfied with good by the fruit of his mouth: and the recompence of a man's hands shall be rendered unto him.

– Proverbs 12:14

127. Delayed decisions extend suffering for yourself and others. Prompt, right, resolute decisions, plus taking action avoid much pain.

Boast not thyself of to morrow; for thou knowest not what a day may bring forth.

– Proverbs 27:1

128. Having a life mission or vision is the key to having overcoming strength and power over opposition. You can overcome life's obstacles when you have something greater to live for than the opposition that challenges you.

Where there is no vision, the people perish:
but he that keepeth the law, happy is he.

– Proverbs 29:18

129. May God's favor prosper you today! May you have peace, (shalom!) in every area of your family, job, business, life, and all that you possess. In Jesus name, amen!

And thus shall ye say to him that liveth in prosperity, Peace be both to thee, and peace be to thine house, and peace be unto all that thou hast.

–1 Samuel 25:6

130. Any place that you can find an unmet need, you will find the seed for financial profit. God is looking for people willing to solve the earth's unmet needs. If you are willing, He will hire you!

If ye be willing and obedient, ye shall eat the good of the land:

– Isaiah 1:19

131. To prepare your meat or provision in the summer of life is exceedingly wise. You don't have to be exceedingly strong or smart, just exceedingly aware of what time it is, and use your time, talents, and resources well.

There be four things which are little upon the earth, but they are exceeding wise: the ants are a people not strong, yet they prepare their meat in the summer.

– Proverbs 30:24–25

132. God is love. He loves everyone. Yet, He has a special love, attachment, and affection for those who love Him back affectionately, obediently, and diligently. He will prove Himself a faithful Rewarder of those who diligently seek and obey Him.

I love them that love me; and those that seek me early shall find me. Riches and honour are with me; yea, durable riches and righteousness. My fruit is better than gold, yea, than fine gold; and my revenue than choice silver. I lead in the way of righteousness, in the midst of the paths of judgment:
that I may cause those that love me to inherit substance; and I will fill their treasures.

– Proverbs 8:17–21

133. The early bird gets the worms. The late bird eats the dust that the early bird left behind!

Seest thou a man diligent in his business?
he shall stand before kings; he shall not stand before mean men.

— Proverbs 22:29

134. God gives everyone the opportunity to prosper. That's His desire above all things, that we prosper and be in health, even as our souls prospers.

He raiseth up the poor out of the dust,
and lifteth up the beggar from the dunghill,
to set them among princes, and to make them inherit the throne of glory: for the pillars of the earth are the Lord's, and he hath set the world upon them.

—1 Samuel 2:8

135. Some say the proof is in the pudding. However, I say the proof is in the putting forth of effort to accomplish your goals. Many wise people proved their worth in life through the putting forth of effort. The attaining of knowledge, plus putting forth practical application, obtains goals.

Yea, a man may say, Thou hast faith, and I have works: shew me thy faith without thy works, and I will shew thee my faith by my works.

— James 2:18

136. Every man and woman is included in God's gift of wealth and riches. It is His gift to give you the true desires of your heart. He's given you the power and ability to get wealth, and accomplish your goals in life. It is the gift of God to you!

Every man also to whom God hath given riches and wealth, and hath given him power to eat thereof, and to take his portion, and to rejoice in his labour; this is the gift of God. For he shall not much remember the days of his life; because God answereth him in the joy of his heart.

– Ecclesiastes 5:19–20

137. How to Be a Hero?

Find something that needs to be done. Then, willingly take the responsibility of actually doing it. It can be just as simple as washing the dishes or shopping for grocery for your family. If it needs to be done, do it!

For if there be first a willing mind, it is accepted according to that a man hath, and not according to that he hath not.

–2 Corinthians 8:12

138.
God has given us the gift of work to enjoy ourselves and to be constructively productive. He desires us to spend our time rejoicing in the work He has given us. It is a means for doing good in life and having daily provision. It is the gift of God to us!

What profit hath he that worketh in that wherein he laboureth? I have seen the travail, which God hath given to the sons of men to be exercised in it. He hath made every thing beautiful in his time: also he hath set the world in their heart, so that no man can find out the work that God maketh from the beginning to the end. I know that there is no good in them, but for a man to rejoice, and to do good in his life. And also that every man should eat and drink, and enjoy the good of all his labour, it is the gift of God.

– Ecclesiastes 3:9–13

139. God is greater than any situation, circumstance, or ordeal on earth. He loves His children, and He desires us all to have long prosperous lives full of His goodness. May God's blessing rest upon our nation. In Jesus name, amen.

Beloved, I wish above all things that thou mayest prosper and be in health, even as thy soul prospereth.

–3 John 1:2

140. The ability to see determines your ability to be. If you can catch a vision of the future God desires for you, you can obtain it. You will progress in the direction of your strongest and clearest vision. Choose your vision carefully by surrounding yourself with pictures of a more desirable future.

Where there is no vision, the people perish:
but he that keepeth the law, happy is he.

– Proverbs 29:18

141. The truths of God's Word have been tested, tried, and proven pure and irrefutable. Those who trust in God's Word and strategically, specifically, and completely obey it will find a sure and trustworthy foundation for their lives.

The law of the Lord is perfect, converting the soul: the testimony of the Lord is sure, making wise the simple. The statutes of the Lord are right, rejoicing the heart: the commandment of the Lord is pure, enlightening the eyes. The fear of the Lord is clean, enduring for ever:
the judgments of the Lord are true and righteous altogether. More to

be desired are they than gold, yea, than much fine gold:
sweeter also than honey and the honeycomb.
Moreover by them is thy servant warned:
and in keeping of them there is great reward.

– Psalm 19:7–11

142. When God plants the seed of a divine idea in the womb of your fertile mind, please allow yourself to conceive the vision He has planted by believing and taking action on it, that you may birth forth a precious, new, and prosperous thing in the earth!

The slothful man roasteth not that which he took in hunting: but the substance of a diligent man is precious.

– Proverbs 12:27

143. Each person's reward in life is granted by God. We can determine what reward we receive by how we choose to live. We should serve and help people, but we should live to please the Lord.

And whatsoever ye do, do it heartily, as to the Lord, and not unto men; knowing that of the Lord ye shall receive the reward of the inheritance: for ye serve the Lord Christ. But he that doeth wrong shall receive for the wrong which he hath done: and there is no respect of persons.

– Colossians 3:23–25

144. Sometimes you have to take big risks in order to gain big rewards. Just like in investing: the greater the risk, plus

opportunity, the greater the potential gain. However, when you step out on God's Word, the reward is guaranteed.

Now when he had left speaking, he said unto Simon, Launch out into the deep, and let down your nets for a draught. And Simon answering said unto him, Master, we have toiled all the night, and have taken nothing: nevertheless at thy word I will let down the net. And when they had this done, they inclosed a great multitude of fishes: and their net brake. And they beckoned unto their partners, which were in the other ship, that they should come and help them. And they came, and filled both the ships, so that they began to sink.

– Luke 5:4–7

145. The quality of your thoughts will determine the quality of your life. You have the power to choose the quality of your thoughts through choosing the quality of your input. The books, television, movies, music, and people you receive from are shaping your thoughts and perspective of reality.

A good man out of the good treasure of his heart bringeth forth that which is good; and an evil man out of the evil treasure of his heart bringeth forth that which is evil: for of the abundance of the heart his mouth speaketh.

– Luke 6:45

146. True love gives wings, not strings, and yet it binds people together through devotion. True love is a free gift.

Many waters cannot quench love, neither can the floods drown it: if a man would give all the substance of his house for love, it would utterly be contemned.

– Song of Solomon 8:7

147. Those who rule and manipulate through the use of fear and violence prove their own fear and weakness.

But he that doeth wrong shall receive for the wrong which he hath done: and there is no respect of persons.

– Colossians 3:25

148. Reality is the only place of change; everything else is a place of pretension and the strange and a prolonging of the pain.

Open rebuke is better than secret love.
Faithful are the wounds of a friend;
but the kisses of an enemy are deceitful.

– Proverbs 27:5–6

149. We only have a relatively short lifetime on earth; thus, we should take account of our use of time, and ask and seek God's favor and blessing on the work of our hands, so that we can enjoy the greatest benefit and pleasure from what we do in it.

So teach us to number our days,
that we may apply our hearts unto wisdom.

– Psalm 90:12

150. I would rather run the risk of being rich than positively possess the peril of being poor.

The Blessing of The Lord, it maketh rich, and He addeth no sorrow with it.

– Proverbs 10:22

151. Fear, anger, and manipulation are unhealthy bases for relationships. All friendships, relationships, business alliances, and associations should be based on willing freedom and mutual respect.

Now the Lord is that Spirit: and where the Spirit of the Lord is, there is liberty.

–2 Corinthians 3:17

152. If you are working to accomplish great deeds— building a business, a career, a family, a great marriage and home, etc.— hold on and be encouraged and be strong. Your work will be rewarded!

Be ye strong therefore, and let not your hands be weak: for your work shall be rewarded.

–2 Chronicles 15:7

153. Passion is the key to successfully accomplishing your goals with joy. Let us finish this year strong, with thankful hearts. As you and I pursue the plans and purpose God has for each of us, let us do it passionately and we will surely accomplish all that He has for us with the spirit of joy!

Go thy way, eat thy bread with joy, and drink thy wine with a merry heart; for God now accepteth thy works. Let thy garments be always white; and let thy head lack no ointment. Live joyfully with the wife whom thou lovest all the days of the life of thy vanity, which he hath given thee under the sun, all the days of thy vanity: for that is thy portion in this life, and in thy labour which thou takest under

the sun. Whatsoever thy hand findeth to do, do it with thy might; for there is no work, nor device, nor knowledge, nor wisdom, in the grave, whither thou goest.

– Ecclesiastes 9:7–10

154. Your diligence on your job will determine your promotion to the next level. Your desire to take on higher responsibility will open the door for your next promotion. Your actions will schedule your next elevation in life.

For promotion cometh neither from the east,
nor from the west, nor from the south.
But God is the judge: he putteth down one, and setteth up another

– Psalm 75:6–7

155. Conceptual understanding is the key to leadership. Functional understanding is the key to management and possibly a job position. The combination of the two creates competent, successful organizations.

Wisdom is the principal thing; therefore get wisdom: and with all thy getting get understanding.

– Proverbs 4:7

156. Live everyday to the full. Enjoy your life to the full today. Be thankful for our daily bread. Be thankful for your job, family, health, and home. Believe God for long life, full of plenty. Nevertheless, be thankful for today's manna!

And when the dew that lay was gone up, behold, upon the face of the wilderness there lay a small round thing, as small as the hoar

frost on the ground. And when the children of Israel saw it, they said one to another, It is manna: for they wist not what it was. And Moses said unto them, This is the bread which the Lord hath given you to eat

– Exodus 16:14–15

157. It only takes an attitude of prayer throughout the day to continually receive the strength of God. Lean your thoughts and spirit toward Him during the day, letting Him know you are depending on Him, and He will always be there to strengthen you.

Thou wilt keep him in perfect peace, whose mind is stayed on thee: because he trusteth in thee. Trust ye in the Lord for ever: for in the Lord JEHOVAH is everlasting strength:

– Isaiah 26:3–4

158. To abandon the Word of God is to abandon our source of life in this fallen world. God's Word is life. Any other source of worldly wisdom is derived from the fallen nature of man.

And Jesus answered him, saying, It is written, That man shall not live by bread alone, but by every word of God.

– Luke 4:4

159. The key to wealth, happiness, and satisfaction in life is to discover and cultivate the resources you have inside. Your inside is your field of discovery.

He that tilleth his land shall be satisfied with bread: but he that followeth vain persons is void of understanding.

– Proverbs 12:11

160. Ultimately those who work hard and smart will be rewarded with leadership and higher responsibility, and a greater degree of success in life.

The hand of the diligent shall bear rule:
but the slothful shall be under tribute.

– Proverbs 12:24

161. Whatever you are doing in striving for excellence, productivity, and profit, what matters most is that you are doing it. There's profit in what you actually do.

In all labour there is profit: but the talk of the lips tendeth only to penury.

– Proverbs 14:23

162. Effectual, fervent prayer and fasting; plus, right living, is never in vain. It always has the power to effect change!

Then came the disciples to Jesus apart, and said, Why could not we cast him out? And Jesus said unto them, Because of your unbelief: for verily I say unto you, If ye have faith as a grain of mustard seed, ye shall say unto this mountain, Remove hence to yonder place; and it shall remove; and nothing shall be impossible unto you. Howbeit this kind goeth not out but by prayer and fasting.

– Matthew 17:19–21

163. Got faith? Got a vision? Got God? Got enough! If God be for us, who can be against us!

What shall we then say to these things? If God be for us, who can be against us?

– Romans 8:31

164. You have the ability to keep yourself happy and encouraged by choosing to walk by faith and not by sight. You can rejoice by choice. God is faithful. You are blessed today. Your tomorrow will produce greater blessings.

The blessing of the Lord, it maketh rich, and he addeth no sorrow with it.

– Proverbs 10:22

165. God desires to show you His way. He desires to reveal His plan to your heart. He is speaking to you through the Bible and prayer. Spend time seeking Him morning and evening. He will answer those who seek Him.

Seek ye the Lord while he may be found,
call ye upon him while he is near:

– Isaiah 55:6

166. Today's prescription, the daily three-word cure for pride, worry, fear, and forgetfulness: Thank You Lord!

Take several times a day, morning, noon, and night. You will feel better instantly.

It is a good thing to give thanks unto the Lord,
and to sing praises unto thy name, O most High: to shew forth thy lovingkindness in the morning, and thy faithfulness every night.

– Psalm 92:1–2

167. When you have a dream, you must surround yourself with those who help to encourage your dream. Connect with people that make your baby leap in the womb of faith! You will see your dream come to pass!

And it came to pass, that, when Elisabeth heard the salutation of Mary, the babe leaped in her womb; and Elisabeth was filled with the Holy Ghost: and she spake out with a loud voice, and said, Blessed art thou among women, and blessed is the fruit of thy womb. And whence is this to me, that the mother of my Lord should come to me? For, lo, as soon as the voice of thy salutation sounded in mine ears, the babe leaped in my womb for joy. And blessed is she that believed: for there shall be a performance of those things which were told her from the Lord.

– Luke 1:41–45

168. This is the season to rejoice! Jesus Christ was born into the earth to give us life and life more abundantly! Joy to the world the Lord has come! He lived. He died in our place on the cross for our sins. He rose again. He lives for us today!

And suddenly there was with the angel a multitude of the heavenly host praising God, and saying, Glory to God in the highest, and on earth peace, good will toward men.

– Luke 2:13–14

169. Today is another opportunity for you to shine by showing your difference in excellence, diligence, and faithfulness. The demonstration of these characteristics is the key to distinction and promotion.

Most men will proclaim every one his own goodness: but a faithful man who can find?

– Proverbs 20:6

170. Christmas is the perfect time to give gifts to those you love. It's the season to express what you have in your heart in a tangible way. A gift, even small in size, may be large enough to change someone's world. God changed our eternal future with the priceless gift of a baby—Jesus Christ, God's only begotten Son.

For unto us a child is born, unto us a son is given: and the government shall be upon his shoulder: and his name shall be called Wonderful, Counsellor, The mighty God,
The everlasting Father, The Prince of Peace.

– Isaiah 9:6

171. To treat others with love, kindness, and fairness is the greatest gift we can give one another and to God this year. How we treat one another will be remembered far longer than any material item.

Thus speaketh the Lord of hosts, saying, Execute true judgment, and shew mercy and compassions every man to his brother: and oppress not the widow, nor the fatherless, the stranger, nor the poor; and let none of you imagine evil against his brother in your heart.

– Zechariah 7:9–10

172. The journey of faith should not mean ignoring today's realities while focusing on tomorrow. Rather, it should be a testament of your awareness and discontent with today's realities, thus being motivated to keep moving as swiftly as possible into a more favorable future.

Let us therefore fear, lest, a promise being left us of entering into his rest, any of you should seem to come short of it.

– Hebrews 4:1

173. You can do all things through Christ, who is giving you strength to do it! You were born for greatness and destined for success in all that you do. Depend on the strength of God today. Ask and receive His strength. His strength is just a prayer away!

Then he answered and spake unto me, saying, This is the word of the Lord unto Zerubbabel, saying, Not by might, nor by power, but by my spirit, saith the Lord of hosts.

– Zechariah 4:6

174. Jesus came to the earth to deliver us from the bondage of sin. He came to free us and empower us to live out His principles. Those who only see Him as a religious figure, while failing to obey His Words, are sadly missing the whole point of Him coming on Christmas Day. He says, "If a man loves Me; he will keep My words."

Therefore whosoever heareth these sayings of mine, and doeth them, I will liken him unto a wise man, which built his house upon a

rock: and the rain descended, and the floods came, and the winds blew, and beat upon that house; and it fell not: for it was founded upon a rock. And every one that heareth these sayings of mine, and doeth them not, shall be likened unto a foolish man, which built his house upon the sand: and the rain descended, and the floods came, and the winds blew, and beat upon that house; and it fell: and great was the fall of it.

– Matthew 7:24–27

175. The system works for those who work it.

In all labour there is profit: but the talk of the lips tendeth only to penury.

– Proverbs 14:23

176. Christmas is a celebration of the greatest Gift given. God, the heavenly Father, gave Jesus Christ, His Holy Son, to deliver us, the rest of His children, from the bondage and estrangement of sin. Now, we have a right and way to reenter our proper relationship with our Father.

For God so loved the world, that he gave his only begotten Son, that whosoever believeth in him should not perish, but have everlasting life. For God sent not his Son into the world to condemn the world; but that the world through him might be saved.

– John 3:16–17

177. In life, there's never any reason to be full of pride or to be intimidated by others. There's no actual superiority or inferiority among people, only differences in knowledge and

experience. We are all made by God, out of the same material: fragile flesh and precious red blood.

The rich and poor meet together: the Lord is the maker of them all.

– Proverbs 22:2

178. Unusual acts of faith on our part activate great acts of miracle working power on God's part!

But without faith it is impossible to please him: for he that cometh to God must believe that he is, and that he is a rewarder of them that diligently seek him.

– Hebrews 11:6

179. Why don't you step out and do something new? Start that business you've been wanting to start. You can do it, if you study for it, like anyone else who has started theirs. If you don't know how to do it, just start studying someone else who has done it already. You will succeed with study, time, and effort!

And that ye study to be quiet, and to do your own business, and to work with your own hands, as we commanded you; that ye may walk honestly toward them that are without, and that ye may have lack of nothing.

–1 Thessalonians 4:11–12

180. Decide to say goodbye to some things today. Leave them on this side of the year. Don't take them into the New Year. Decide what you want to be and become in the New

Year. Make a plan and follow the steps for change. A new year is a new opportunity for change and improvement.

The steps of a good man are ordered by the Lord: and he delighteth in his way.

– Psalm 37:23

181. The wisdom of preparation is that it makes the hard work of application and execution easier. Whatever you are trying to accomplish this year, be sure to have prepared, through study and practice; you will surely be guided to a greater success.

If the iron be blunt, and he do not whet the edge, then must he put to more strength: but wisdom is profitable to direct.

– Ecclesiastes 10:10

182. Once you can think your way out, you can work your way out. Riches start with a state of mind.

For as he thinketh in his heart, so is he:
Eat and drink, saith he to thee;
but his heart is not with thee.

– Proverbs 23:7

183. This year is the year of change. This is your opportunity to have what you have been believing for. No matter how difficult your past, your now can be better. The current of favor and advantage is moving in the direction of the believers. Jump in! This is your year of opportunity. This is your opportunity to make change for a better future.

Whatsoever thy hand findeth to do, do it with thy might; for there is no work, nor device, nor knowledge, nor wisdom, in the grave, whither thou goest. I returned, and saw under the sun, that the race is not to the swift, nor the battle to the strong, neither yet bread to the wise, nor yet riches to men of understanding, nor yet favour to men of skill; but time and chance happeneth to them all.

– Ecclesiastes 9:10–11

184. A mouth can say many things, but love says it all. Just like faith without works is dead, love without actions is ineffective!
As the old people used to say, "Love is what love does!"

For in Jesus Christ neither circumcision availeth any thing, nor uncircumcision; but faith which worketh by love.

– Galatians 5:6

For as the body without the spirit is dead, so faith without works is dead also.

– James 2:26

185. Most typical relationships and human interactions are prone to brinksmanship and one-upmanship; however, the sincere behavior of honesty should be based on love and mutual goodwill.

Who is a wise man and endued with knowledge among you? let him shew out of a good conversation his works with meekness of wisdom. But if ye have bitter envying and strife in your hearts, glory not, and lie not against the truth. This wisdom descendeth not from above, but is earthly, sensual, devilish. For where envying and strife is, there is confusion and every evil work. But the wisdom that is

from above is first pure, then peaceable, gentle, and easy to be intreated, full of mercy and good fruits, without partiality, and without hypocrisy. And the fruit of righteousness is sown in peace of them that make peace.

– James 3:13–18

186. The Bible is the Word of God. It is God talking to you and me. We will find comfort, peace, wisdom, and direction from spending time studying it everyday.

Come unto me, all ye that labour and are heavy laden, and I will give you rest. Take my yoke upon you, and learn of me; for I am meek and lowly in heart: and ye shall find rest unto your souls. For my yoke is easy, and my burden is light.

– Matthew 11:28–30

187. Faith is a process. The steps of faith plus time equals success.

That ye be not slothful, but followers of them who through faith and patience inherit the promises.

– Hebrews 6:12

188. Good success is the result of learning the principles of God's Word and obeying them. The Word of God is anointed to destroy the yoke of poverty and failure. Obeying God's principles guarantees good success.

This book of the law shall not depart out of thy mouth; but thou shalt meditate therein day and night, that thou mayest observe to do according to all that is written therein: for then thou shalt make thy way prosperous, and then thou shalt have good success.

– Joshua 1:8

189. Singing and worship are important keys and miraculous means of drawing the presence of the Creator— God and Father of our Lord Jesus Christ— into your life and environment. He doesn't discriminate among those that worship and obey Him. Take time to sing and worship; it will bring peace to your situation.

For thus saith the high and lofty One
that inhabiteth eternity, whose name is Holy;
I dwell in the high and holy place,
with him also that is of a contrite and humble spirit, to revive the spirit of the humble,
and to revive the heart of the contrite ones.

– Isaiah 57:15

190. Marriage is an opportunity to practice the best of your love on someone personally. In fact, each of our relationships and interactions with people gives us the opportunity to exercise the love that we have in our hearts. God put love in your heart so you can give it away to others.

Love endures long and is patient and kind; love never is envious nor boils over with jealousy, is not boastful or vainglorious, does not display itself haughtily.
It is not conceited (arrogant and inflated with pride); it is not rude (unmannerly) and does not act unbecomingly. Love (God's love in us) does not insist on its own rights or its own way, for it is not self-seeking; it is not touchy or fretful or resentful; it takes no account of the evil done to it [it pays no attention to a suffered wrong].
It does not rejoice at injustice and unrighteousness, but rejoices when right and truth prevail.

Love bears up under anything and everything that comes, is ever ready to believe the best of every person, its hopes are fadeless under all circumstances, and it endures everything [without weakening].
Love never fails [never fades out or becomes obsolete or comes to an end]. As for prophecy ([a]the gift of interpreting the divine will and purpose), it will be fulfilled and pass away; as for tongues, they will be destroyed and cease; as for knowledge, it will pass away [it will lose its value and be superseded by truth].

–1 Corinthians 13:4–8
(AMP)

191. King David was a great man. However, he was first of all a worshiper. He was a shepherd boy that became a king. Yet, at his core, he was a worshiper. Some people become important and great, but they quit worshipping the God that made them great. Worship is the cure for pride and the sustaining of greatness.

Now these be the last words of David.
David the son of Jesse said, and the man who was raised up on high, the anointed of the God of Jacob, and the sweet psalmist of Israel, said, The Spirit of the Lord spake by me, and his word was in my tongue.

–2 Samuel 23:1–2

192. Whether in the area of health, finances, relationships, or other, do the practical while believing God for the miraculous. Go to the doctor. Make a budget. Trust, but verify. Then keep an open heart for God to exceed your natural efforts and expectations.

The simple believeth every word: but the prudent man looketh well to his going.

– Proverbs 14:15

193. A wise doctor once said concerning patients, "Always listen to the person's heart." We too must be patient enough to always listen to a person's heart in relationships.

He that answereth a matter before he heareth it, it is folly and shame unto him.

– Proverbs 18:13

194. How to solve a problem is in many cases determined based on who you take your problem to. If you take your car to a mechanic, you may need a new motor. If you take it to a car salesman, you will need a new car. If you go to a surgeon, you will need surgery. If you go to a dentist, you will need a root canal. If you go to a pastor, you will need prayer. If you go to a funeral director, you will need a funeral. If you go to God, you will find your answer!

There is no [human] wisdom or understanding or counsel [that can prevail] against the Lord.

– Proverbs 21:30
(AMP)

195. Maximize your gifts; then, invest in your ideas. Become skillful and profitable with your God-given gifts; then invest that profit in your God-given ideas. This is a key to becoming a self-made millionaire or billionaire.

Wherefore I perceive that there is nothing better, than that a man should rejoice in his own works; for that is his portion: for who shall bring him to see what shall be after him?

– Ecclesiastes 3:22

196. Small people seek to control other people. Big people seek to free other people to be big too.

Not for that we have dominion over your faith, but are helpers of your joy: for by faith ye stand.

–2 Corinthians 1:24

197. Focus less on fixing the past; and rather, focus on flourishing, thriving, and profiting in your now today. And prepare to enjoy a more prosperous future.

Now faith is the substance of things hoped for, the evidence of things not seen.

– Hebrews 11:1

198. God is not just the God of miracles; He is the God of lifestyle. He wants you and me to live the lifestyle of "the blessing." God tells us to give tithes and offerings so He can bless us with the lifestyle of the blessing. The miracle of the blessing is continual, gradual, sustainable increase and protection that lasts from generation to generation, and to children's children.

Bring ye all the tithes into the storehouse, that there may be meat in mine house, and prove me now herewith, saith the Lord of hosts, if I will not open you the windows of heaven, and pour you out a

blessing, that there shall not be room enough to receive it. And I will rebuke the devourer for your sakes, and he shall not destroy the fruits of your ground; neither shall your vine cast her fruit before the time in the field, saith the Lord of hosts. And all nations shall call you blessed: for ye shall be a delightsome land, saith the Lord of hosts.

– Malachi 3:10–12

199. There are many endeavors in which we may spend our time, but the most crucial endeavor is that of seeking and obtaining the wisdom necessary to successfully navigate the waters of life; and in doing so, we must take time to get a full understanding.

Get wisdom, get understanding: forget it not; neither decline from the words of my mouth.
Forsake her not, and she shall preserve thee:
love her, and she shall keep thee. Wisdom is the principal thing; therefore get wisdom: and with all thy getting get understanding.

– Proverbs 4:5–7

200. On Valentine's Day here's a very biblical thing that every husband can do for our wives that won't cost anymore than a cup of coffee: He-brews.

Marriage is honourable in all, and the bed undefiled: but whoremongers and adulterers God will judge.

– Hebrews 13:4

201. Ultimately, there are no limits to our success but the limits we put on ourselves. Excuses never hold up in the final analysis, only results. We can—if we only will. Period.

I can do all things through Christ which strengtheneth me.

– Philippians 4:13

202. The key to time mastery is to focus on making everyday produce a masterpiece exemplifying your purpose in life. Make your moments count for something that reveals the treasure inside of you, and lasts beyond you.

So teach us to number our days, that we may apply our hearts unto wisdom.

– Psalm 90:12

203. The Bible is the story of imperfect people in imperfect situations responding to a perfect God to accomplish His perfect plan— in spite of our imperfections and through His Grace.

And Salmon begat Booz of Rachab; and Booz begat Obed of Ruth; and Obed begat Jesse; and Jesse begat David the king; and David the king begat Solomon of her that had been the wife of Urias.

– Matthew 1:5–6

204. Well, well, well. It is well with my soul! It is well with my health! It is well with my wealth! Well, well, well!

Beloved, I wish above all things that thou mayest prosper and be in health, even as thy soul prospereth.

–3 John 1:2

205. When you know that you are the dye in the water, it doesn't matter who refuses to recognize you. Your influence can never be denied.

Another parable spake he unto them; The kingdom of heaven is like unto leaven, which a woman took, and hid in three measures of meal, till the whole was leavened.

– Matthew 13:33

206. Adversity is good. It gives you the opportunity to prevail against the status quo. It is your opportunity to stand out against the prevailing conditions.

If thou faint in the day of adversity, thy strength is small.

– Proverbs 24:10

207. Striving to obey God's laws for living in this earth with one another should be our fervent, full-time occupation. In doing so, we will find peace, harmony, and a happy, fulfilled life.

Thus speaketh the Lord of hosts, saying, Execute true judgment, and shew mercy and compassions every man to his brother: and oppress not the widow, nor the fatherless, the stranger, nor the poor; and let none of you imagine evil against his brother in your heart.

– Zechariah 7:9–10

208. When it seems like life is too much and you feel like your faith is swaying, don't give up. Tie a knot in the rope of

hope and hold on.
Tie a knot in the rope of hope and hold on!

The righteous also shall hold on his way,
and he that hath clean hands shall be stronger and stronger.

– Job 17:9

209. God has not given us the spirit of fear, but of power, and of love, and of a sound, calm, stable, disciplined, well-balanced mind.

For God hath not given us the spirit of fear; but of power, and of love, and of a sound mind.

–2 Timothy 1:7

210. After a while, people who talk too much, you can't hear, until they actually do something worth talking about.

For a dream cometh through the multitude of business; and a fool's voice is known by multitude of words.

– Ecclesiastes 5:3

211. Every time we have a need, God will give us an opportunity to sow a seed. A seed of love produces more love. A seed of money to those in need produces more money for your time of need. A seed of comfort to those in pain produces relief in your times of trouble. Give a seed out of your time of need; it will produce a harvest of supply.

Give, and it shall be given unto you; good measure, pressed down, and shaken together, and running over, shall men give into your

bosom. For with the same measure that ye mete withal it shall be measured to you again.

– Luke 6:38

212. Through humility, enthusiasm, and positivity we can wholeheartedly possess the blessing, which God is offering to us each day. We must condition our hearts to receive it through prayer, worship, and meditating His Word.

By humility and the fear of the Lord
are riches, and honour, and life.

– Proverbs 22:4

213. No matter how much knowledge, skill, or acumen we are able to gain and operate in through natural means, the Word of God will always be the source of eternal life, truth, and stability.

And Jesus answered him, saying, It is written, That man shall not live by bread alone, but by every word of God.

– Luke 4:4

214. Leaders are readers. Workers take instructions.

Wisdom is the principal thing; therefore get wisdom: and with all thy getting get understanding.

– Proverbs 4:7

215. Your chief daily goal should be doing and finishing. Only what you finish will you be paid for ultimately.

So teach us to number our days, that we may apply our hearts unto wisdom.

– Psalm 90:12

216. God doesn't lead us into the valley of possibilities. He directs us into the path of positivities. He is positive about what He has preplanned for you to accomplish. It's up to us to believe that it is possible.

For we are his workmanship, created in Christ Jesus unto good works, which God hath before ordained that we should walk in them.

– Ephesians 2:10

217. Live one life at a time. *Your own*!

But let every man prove his own work, and then shall he have rejoicing in himself alone, and not in another.

– Galatians 6:4

218. The snow is God's blanket for the earth to take a nap. There are treasures in the snow.

Hast thou entered into the treasures of the snow? or hast thou seen the treasures of the hail, which I have reserved against the time of trouble, against the day of battle and war?

– Job 38:22–23

219. It's not what you learn when you were made to learn that makes the grandest difference. It is what you decide to

master after the compulsory period that proves the effectiveness of that compulsory period. The addition of further personal pursuit determines your ultimate success.

Give instruction to a wise man, and he will be yet wiser: teach a just man, and he will increase in learning.

– Proverbs 9:9

220. God is our refuge from the storms of life. He is our strength during times of trial. He is a very present help in the midst of our trouble!

For thou hast been a strength to the poor,
a strength to the needy in his distress,
a refuge from the storm, a shadow from the heat, when the blast of the terrible ones is as a storm against the wall.

– Isaiah 25:4

221. As we feed our mind the right things, we make saying the right things easier. As it has been said, "You are what you eat." If you put the right things in, the right things will come out.

A good man out of the good treasure of his heart bringeth forth that which is good; and an evil man out of the evil treasure of his heart bringeth forth that which is evil: for of the abundance of the heart his mouth speaketh.

– Luke 6:45

222. Favor, goodness, opportunity, and better chances are guaranteed to those who continually seek and do the good

things God desires and requires. We only must look for it and take advantage of it.

He that diligently seeketh good procureth favour: but he that seeketh mischief, it shall come unto him.

– Proverbs 11:27

223. We must keep track of how we spend our money and time. A budget and spending record records our financial efforts. A calendar, planner, and event record records our use of time. These are the days of our lives!

So teach us to number our days,
that we may apply our hearts unto wisdom.

– Psalm 90:12

224. Dreams can be dangerous. They require a lot of hard work, risk, and effort even before they can be seen by others. Dreams and dreamers also can attract attack by non-dreamers. However, dreamers save the world!

And Joseph dreamed a dream, and he told it his brethren: and they hated him yet the more. And he said unto them, Hear, I pray you, this dream which I have dreamed: for, behold, we were binding sheaves in the field, and, lo, my sheaf arose, and also stood upright; and, behold, your sheaves stood round about, and made obeisance to my sheaf. And his brethren said to him, Shalt thou indeed reign over us? or shalt thou indeed have dominion over us? And they hated him yet the more for his dreams, and for his words.

– Genesis 37:5–8

225. Life is filled with pressing priorities. We often have to choose which we will do first. Jobs, bills, business, etc., usually won't wait. Therefore, we have to give them their due

attention. But don't forget to save the best of yourself for your family, loved ones, and home.

Prepare thy work without, and make it fit for thyself in the field; and afterwards build thine house.

– Proverbs 24:27

226. Successful people make progress. Unsuccessful people make excuses.

For a dream cometh through the multitude of business; and a fool's voice is known by multitude of words.

– Ecclesiastes 5:3

227. We can trust our ability to think right thoughts and make good decisions as we renew our minds to godly thinking.

The thoughts of the righteous are right: but the counsels of the wicked are deceit.

– Proverbs 12:5

228. Life is too short to not celebrate often!

And God saw every thing that he had made, and, behold, it was very good. And the evening and the morning were the sixth day.

– Genesis 1:31

229. Jesus overcame the adversity of a fallen world. They that are in Christ Jesus have also overcome the adversity of

the world. We must abide in Him, and stand resolute, and rest in that victory!

For whatsoever is born of God overcometh the world: and this is the victory that overcometh the world, even our faith. Who is he that overcometh the world, but he that believeth that Jesus is the Son of God?

−1 John 5:4–5

230. God hears your prayers today. He delights in you. And he delights in hearing you call on Him. Whoever calls on the Lord today shall be saved!

But what saith it? The word is nigh thee, even in thy mouth, and in thy heart: that is, the word of faith, which we preach; that if thou shalt confess with thy mouth the Lord Jesus, and shalt believe in thine heart that God hath raised him from the dead, thou shalt be saved. For with the heart man believeth unto righteousness; and with the mouth confession is made unto salvation. For the scripture saith, Whosoever believeth on him shall not be ashamed. For there is no difference between the Jew and the Greek: for the same Lord over all is rich unto all that call upon him. For whosoever shall call upon the name of the Lord shall be saved.

− Romans 10:8–13

231. The value of telling the truth is that truth can withstand the force of time and change. You will have the security of knowing you fully expressed the truth, even when circumstances change.

The lip of truth shall be established for ever:
but a lying tongue is but for a moment.

– Proverbs 12:19

232. I can't afford to fail. And, it's not over until I win!

Brethren, I count not myself to have apprehended: but this one thing I do, forgetting those things which are behind, and reaching forth unto those things which are before, I press toward the mark for the prize of the high calling of God in Christ Jesus.

– Philippians 3:13–14

233. Today is a day of victory! There is victory over adversity; victory over sickness; victory over depression; victory over lack. Today is the day that the Lord has made for you and I to rejoice and be glad in the victory He won for us on the Cross! Have a wonderful day!

This is the Lord's doing;
it is marvellous in our eyes.
This is the day which the Lord hath made;
we will rejoice and be glad in it.
Save now, I beseech thee, O Lord:
O Lord, I beseech thee, send now prosperity.

– Psalm 118:23–25

234. It is wise for a man and a woman to fall in love, get married, and begin to build a family together. This is God's ageless, precious gift to humanity. Through gaining an understanding and acceptance of one another's personality differences, the home will be established and made stable. However, only through the increase of practical, usable knowledge will their home be filled with wealth and riches.

Through wisdom is an house builded;
and by understanding it is established:
and by knowledge shall the chambers be filled
with all precious and pleasant riches.

– Proverbs 24:3–4

235. Hurdles are an indication that you are on the right track.

If thou faint in the day of adversity, thy strength is small.

– Proverbs 24:10

236. Many people misjudge a story in the making. They fail to look pass initial circumstances and appearances, to see the ultimate outcome. We should catch a vision of our future, as well as others, and know that the end will be one of prosperity, success, and peace.

Mark the perfect man, and behold the upright: for the end of that man is peace.

– Psalm 37:37

237. The difference between successful people and those who have failed to obtain success is the discipline of obtaining knowledge or the failure to do so. Failure is a curable disease. Knowledge and application are the cure.

My people are destroyed for lack of knowledge: because thou hast rejected knowledge, I will also reject thee, that thou shalt be no priest to me: seeing thou hast forgotten the law of thy God, I will also forget thy children.

– Hosea 4:6

238. The world will keep going round, whether you keep trying to run it or not. You have to know when to get off the merry-go-round and rest a while.

Thus the heavens and the earth were finished, and all the host of them. And on the seventh day God ended his work which he had made; and he rested on the seventh day from all his work which he had made.

– Genesis 2:1–2

239. Rome wasn't built in a day, but it was built everyday. Whatever God has given you to do, keep on working on it until it's done.

The hand of the diligent shall bear rule: but the slothful shall be under tribute.

– Proverbs 12:24

240. It is futile to argue with God. He gives us the privilege to use good sense and choose His way. Yet, ultimately, He never changes in His principles throughout eternity.

Then Job answered and said, I know it is so of a truth: but how should man be just with God?
If he will contend with him, he cannot answer him one of a thousand. He is wise in heart, and mighty in strength: who hath hardened himself against him, and hath prospered?

– Job 9:1–4

241. It may take a moment of inspiration to conceive a dream. But, it may take years of perspiration to bring it to pass. However, if we do not faint in the process, we will see the dream come to pass.

For a dream cometh through the multitude of business; and a fool's voice is known by multitude of words.

– Ecclesiastes 5:3

242. Inspiration plus education equals the information necessary to accomplish your dream. Get it!

Wisdom is the principal thing; therefore get wisdom: and with all thy getting get understanding.

– Proverbs 4:7

243. Education minus creativity, independence, and inspiration equals a potential job. Education plus creativity, independence, and inspiration equals increased potential for being independently wealthy.

Go to the ant, thou sluggard; consider her ways, and be wise: which having no guide, overseer, or ruler, provideth her meat in the summer, and gathereth her food in the harvest.

– Proverbs 6:6–8

244. Life can be difficult, filled with various challenges and demands of varying degrees. However, there is a God! He is the great moderator in the sky! He knows how to govern the earth. He knows how to gauge each of our levels of difficulty. And most importantly, He knows how and when to deliver.

There hath no temptation taken you but such as is common to man: but God is faithful, who will not suffer you to be tempted above that ye are able; but will with the temptation also make a way to escape, that ye may be able to bear it.

–1 Corinthians 10:13

245. We must build up our faith to take action by reading, studying, and speaking God's Word (the Bible). We must discipline and devote ourselves to obey it through prayer and fasting. Then we must act on our faith in order to receive the reward!

And Jesus said unto them, Because of your unbelief: for verily I say unto you, If ye have faith as a grain of mustard seed, ye shall say unto this mountain, Remove hence to yonder place; and it shall remove; and nothing shall be impossible unto you. Howbeit this kind goeth not out but by prayer and fasting.

– Matthew 17:20–21

246. Do not be nervous in the fight. Be stable. Be strong. Be steadfast. Be secure. The Lord is faithful. He will uphold you. He will maintain your cause. He will protect you from the storm. Be secure in Him. He will never fail you.

But the Lord is faithful, who shall stablish you, and keep you from evil.

–2 Thessalonians 3:3

247. Live your life all in! Put all your chips on your future. Live your life today like you really believe for a jackpot future! They that sow abundantly today will receive an abundant harvest tomorrow!

They that sow in tears shall reap in joy.
He that goeth forth and weepeth, bearing precious seed, shall doubtless come again with rejoicing, bringing his sheaves with him.

– Psalm 126:5–6

248. All of our lives, we will be dealing with imperfect people, with our imperfect selves; therefore, we should understand their imperfections.

Put on therefore, as the elect of God, holy and beloved, bowels of mercies, kindness, humbleness of mind, meekness, longsuffering; forbearing one another, and forgiving one another, if any man have a quarrel against any: even as Christ forgave you, so also do ye.

– Colossians 3:12–13

249. If you've been in church for years, listening to the Word, yet, you haven't seen your blessing come through. That may be a sign you need to get up off your "Blessed Assurance" and start something! God's Word will work for those who work it!

What doth it profit, my brethren, though a man say he hath faith, and have not works? can faith save him? Even so faith, if it hath not works, is dead, being alone.

– James 2:14, 17

250. The key to our own deliverance is to focus on the deliverance of others. The key to God helping us is our commitment to help others.

And the Lord turned the captivity of Job, when he prayed for his friends: also the Lord gave Job twice as much as he had before.

– Job 42:10

251. People who fail to take time to get extra in life also fail to endure long enough to take advantage of the big opportunities that come along. We must take time to fill

ourselves with extra oil by spending time with God's Word and prayer in the morning, so we don't burn out before evening.

Then shall the kingdom of heaven be likened unto ten virgins, which took their lamps, and went forth to meet the bridegroom. And five of them were wise, and five were foolish. They that were foolish took their lamps, and took no oil with them: but the wise took oil in their vessels with their lamps.

– Matthew 25:1–4

252. Jesus is the reason for this season too. Jesus is the only begotten Son of God. He came to save the entire world from our sins. As we celebrate Easter, let us remember the life, death, burial, and resurrection of the Lord Jesus Christ as the only payment for our sins.

And the angel said unto her, Fear not, Mary: for thou hast found favour with God. And, behold, thou shalt conceive in thy womb, and bring forth a son, and shalt call his name JESUS. He shall be great, and shall be called the Son of the Highest: and the Lord God shall give unto him the throne of his father David: and he shall reign over the house of Jacob for ever; and of his kingdom there shall be no end.

– Luke 1:30–33

253. Success in any area starts with a made-up mind. There have been people who have done so much more than average, simply because they had a made-up mind, and determination to step out and start with what they had. Go for it today with what you do have. God will bless it!

Now therefore perform the doing of it; that as there was a readiness to will, so there may be a performance also out of that which ye have. For if there be first a willing mind, it is accepted according to that a man hath, and not according to that he hath not.

–2 Corinthians 8:11–12

254. The devil has no new tricks. If you are experiencing what seems to be unexplainable adversity or odd opposition, it is just the same old Devil, trying to steal your blessing. Your blessing is right on your doorstep. Resist the Devil. Expose him for the thief that he is, and don't let him steal your blessing.

The thief cometh not, but for to steal, and to kill, and to destroy: I am come that they might have life, and that they might have it more abundantly.

– John 10:10

255. Believe that you have what it takes to thrive! Not just survive. Jesus came that you might have life and life more abundantly! Live it!

The thief cometh not, but for to steal, and to kill, and to destroy: I am come that they might have life, and that they might have it more abundantly.

– John 10:10

256. When we consistently carry out God's principles for successful living, the end result will always be prosperity. However, we cannot skip the steps and still be blessed.

A faithful man shall abound with blessings: but he that maketh haste to be rich shall not be innocent.

– Proverbs 28:20

257. The Bible is the source of God's wisdom. However, there are books that contain the principles of God lived out in people's lives. If you want to be a doctor, you must study medicine; but the principle of diligence still applies.

Wisdom is the principal thing; therefore get wisdom: and with all thy getting get understanding.

– Proverbs 4:7

258. Many will try to exploit the value you bring without giving you the credit you deserve. The key to being properly rewarded is accurate self-appraisal.

It is naught, it is naught, saith the buyer:
but when he is gone his way, then he boasteth.

– Proverbs 20:14

259. Each day, we should focus our energy and intention upon fulfilling God's destiny for our lives. If you and I are fulfilling what God said for us to do, we will always be successful. Daily obedience equals a lifetime of success.

But seek ye first the kingdom of God, and his righteousness; and all these things shall be added unto you.

– Matthew 6:33

260. Use your own wood, to build your own ship, to sail across your own sea; and don't depend upon riding with someone else.

But let every man prove his own work, and then shall he have rejoicing in himself alone, and not in another.

– Galatians 6:4

261. The same faith that caused you to do other things is the same faith that will cause you to do everything. We are the just. We walk by faith, and not by sight. We are the just. The just shall live by faith!

For we walk by faith, not by sight.

–2 Corinthians 5:7

262. It is not the dream that comforts and rocks you to sleep at night that will change your life; no, it is the dream that wakes you early in morning, burning in your soul, that will put running in your feet, purpose in your life, and the passionate achievement of your destiny!

And the Lord answered me, and said,
Write the vision, and make it plain upon tables, that he may run that readeth it. For the vision is yet for an appointed time,
but at the end it shall speak, and not lie:
though it tarry, wait for it; because it will surely come, it will not tarry. Behold, his soul which is lifted up is not upright in him: but the just shall live by *his* faith.

– Habakkuk 2:2–4

263. The more end-of-the-world events we successfully make it through, and the more God proves that He will always walk us through, the more our confidence will increase to walk through any new challenge.

There hath no temptation taken you but such as is common to man: but God is faithful, who will not suffer you to be tempted above that ye are able; but will with the temptation also make a way to escape, that ye may be able to bear it.

–1 Corinthians 10:13

264. The eternal Creator God is all-wise, all-knowing, all-powerful, and all-loving. He will never fail you. He knows all things regarding your life. He is the Author and the Finisher of your faith. He will help you finish strong!

Be strong and courageous, be not afraid nor dismayed for the king of Assyria, nor for all the multitude that is with him: for there be more with us than with him: with him is an arm of flesh; but with us is the Lord our God to help us, and to fight our battles. And the people rested themselves upon the words of Hezekiah king of Judah.

–2 Chronicles 32:7–8

265. There is power in singing songs of worship, praise, and thanksgiving to God, your Creator, because He is good. He opened your eyes this morning and let you see the beautiful sunshine. It is Him that protects you during the day. Praise Him! You will feel better!

It is a good thing to give thanks unto the Lord,
and to sing praises unto thy name, O most High: to shew forth thy lovingkindness in the morning, and thy faithfulness every night

– Psalm 92:1–2

266. Once you recognize and accept your destiny, as long as you keep on moving in the right direction, you will never be late. If you stay where life is moving, you will move with life!

For to him that is joined to all the living there is hope: for a living dog is better than a dead lion.

– Ecclesiastes 9:4

267. People attack what they are afraid of. People are not afraid of what they are greater than. What people are greater than, they are not afraid of. People attack what is greater than them.

And in nothing terrified by your adversaries: which is to them an evident token of perdition, but to you of salvation, and that of God.

– Philippians 1:28

268. The gift that God gave you will sparkle and prosper wherever you go. It is like a diamond ring on your finger; it sparkles in different ways, according to how the light of life hits you!

A gift is as a precious stone in the eyes of him that hath it: whithersoever it turneth, it prospereth.

– Proverbs 17:8

269. If you want to please God to the highest level, God desires that you grow, improve, and develop in your mind, will, emotions, personality, and intellect so that He can get the

highest use out of your life, and you can live the most prosperous, abundant life!

Beloved, I wish above all things that thou mayest prosper and be in health, even as thy soul prospereth.

–3 John 1:2

270. If we would seek God early and diligently, making Him our God and Rock—if we would live a pure and righteous life before Him—then certainly He will work for us and make all that we have a right to in life prosperous. Though we may start off small, yet we will end up greatly blessed!

If thou wouldest seek unto God betimes,
and make thy supplication to the Almighty; if thou wert pure and upright; surely now he would awake for thee, and make the habitation of thy righteousness prosperous. Though thy beginning was small, yet thy latter end should greatly increase.

– Job 8:5–7

271. The way to deal with the demands of life, is not "Don't worry, be happy". Rather, it is, "Don't worry, get busy!" Take care of the actual requirements of the demand. After you've done what's required, leave it in the Lord's hands.

Wherefore take unto you the whole armour of God, that ye may be able to withstand in the evil day, and having done all, to stand.

– Ephesians 6:13

272. The Word of God is your source of supernatural strength in every situation. Take time to hear the Word of

God by reading His Word aloud from the Bible, so that your own spirit can hear the Word of God coming from your own mouth. You will believe it. You will accept it. You will be strengthened!

And said, O man greatly beloved, fear not: peace be unto thee, be strong, yea, be strong. And when he had spoken unto me, I was strengthened, and said, Let my lord speak; for thou hast strengthened me.

– Daniel 10:19

273. The wisdom of God exceeds the value of a college education. But a college education enhances the value of the Word of God.

Wisdom is the principal thing; therefore get wisdom: and with all thy getting get understanding.

– Proverbs 4:7

274. If you will live like you are planning to live, you will live. Eat right. Exercise. Live holy. Forgive others and yourself. Live like you're planning to live, and you will live.

My son, forget not my law; but let thine heart keep my commandments: for length of days, and long life, and peace, shall they add to thee.

– Proverbs 3:1–2

275. God's grace is greater than any difficulty, challenge, obstacle, failure, or foe you may have to face. Call on His name. He will save you. He can and will deliver you from

your ordeal. He will wash away your sins. He will justify your future. He will give you victory! His name is Jesus Christ. Call Him today!

For whosoever shall call upon the name of the Lord shall be saved.

– Romans 10:13

276. Humility reduces hostility

Only by pride cometh contention: but with the well advised is wisdom.

– Proverbs 13:10

277. We've had the weekend to readjust our thinking. Now it's time to go forth victoriously into another week. God is for us, with us, and in us. He will help us to triumph and prevail in every situation this week.

Now thanks be unto God, which always causeth us to triumph in Christ, and maketh manifest the savour of his knowledge by us in every place.

–2 Corinthians 2:14

278. God will use the natural gifts, skills, and occupation we are accustomed to in order to meet our natural needs. However, when we make meeting His needs our goal, He will release His supernatural power and provision.

And when they were come to Capernaum, they that received tribute money came to Peter, and said, Doth not your master pay tribute? He saith, Yes. And when he was come into the house, Jesus

prevented him, saying, What thinkest thou, Simon? of whom do the kings of the earth take custom or tribute? of their own children, or of strangers? Peter saith unto him, Of strangers. Jesus saith unto him, Then are the children free. Notwithstanding, lest we should offend them, go thou to the sea, and cast an hook, and take up the fish that first cometh up; and when thou hast opened his mouth, thou shalt find a piece of money: that take, and give unto them for me and thee.

– Matthew 17:24–27

279. Today is another opportunity for progressive individuals to excel. You are the saviors of change right where you are. You are the cure for the afflictions within the body of humanity. Today is another opportunity to share progressive change.

Ye are the light of the world. A city that is set on an hill cannot be hid. Neither do men light a candle, and put it under a bushel, but on a candlestick; and it giveth light unto all that are in the house. Let your light so shine before men, that they may see your good works, and glorify your Father which is in heaven.

– Matthew 5:14–16

280. No matter what may be going on in society, no matter the situation, stay focused on fulfilling what God's Word says. Obey daily—moment by moment, decision by decision, word by word— and you will receive the reward of obedience.

But without faith it is impossible to please him: for he that cometh to God must believe that he is, and that he is a rewarder of them that diligently seek him.

– Hebrews 11:6

281. Our job everyday is to walk uprightly before God and obey His Word in every situation. God is love. Let us all fulfill His heart.

He hath shewed thee, O man, what is good;
and what doth the Lord require of thee, but to do justly, and to love mercy, and to walk humbly with thy God?

– Micah 6:8

282. God often gives us opportunities to choose life or death, yes or no, victory or success. Though He is often silent during the examination, it is an open-book test. The book is the Bible.

For this commandment which I command thee this day, it is not hidden from thee, neither is it far off. It is not in heaven, that thou shouldest say, Who shall go up for us to heaven, and bring it unto us, that we may hear it, and do it? Neither is it beyond the sea, that thou shouldest say, Who shall go over the sea for us, and bring it unto us, that we may hear it, and do it? But the word is very nigh unto thee, in thy mouth, and in thy heart, that thou mayest do it.

– Deuteronomy 30:11–14

283. Great gifts are often stored in hardened shells, forgotten wastelands, and unrefined conditions; yet good treasure hunters always seem to find them. Jesus has been searching for you. Only He knows your true value.

Again, the kingdom of heaven is like unto a merchant man, seeking goodly pearls: who, when he had found one pearl of great price, went and sold all that he had, and bought it.

— Matthew 13:45–46

284. Inconveniences and unscheduled delays can be very irritating. Trying situations can test your patience. These are the "fruit inspections" of life that reveal the quality of the fruit of your spirit.

But the fruit of the Spirit is love, joy, peace, longsuffering, gentleness, goodness, faith, meekness, temperance: against such there is no law.

— Galatians 5:22–23

285. We often fear one another: the rich fear the poor, and the poor often fear the rich. Yet, we are all in need of the same thing, made in the image of the same one, true and living God! Love is the great equalizer of all. Love casts out all fear and separation.

The rich and poor meet together: the Lord is the maker of them all.

— Proverbs 22:2

286. Take time daily to prepare yourself through reading the Bible, prayer, and worship, for life will soon put a demand on you. You must be able to answer the demand!

Gird up thy loins now like a man: I will demand of thee, and declare thou unto me.

— Job 40:7

287. Serving the Lord pays off. Those who worship and serve the Lord in righteousness and truth will receive the

harvest of mercy, favor, compassion, and untold blessings in this life and in the life to come.

For since the beginning of the world men have not heard, nor perceived by the ear, neither hath the eye seen, O God, beside thee, what he hath prepared for him that waiteth for him.

– Isaiah 64:4

288. There is never any limitation or restrictions placed on walking in the virtues of God's love. You can never be too loving to others. You could never forgive too much. You could never be too patient. And you could never have too much joy! Live in God's Spirit today. There are no limits.

But the fruit of the Spirit is love, joy, peace, longsuffering, gentleness, goodness, faith, meekness, temperance: against such there is no law.

– Galatians 5:22–23

289. No matter where you may be, and no matter what you may be doing, if you have the favor of God, because of your diligence and excellence, you will always be prosperous.

And the Lord was with Joseph, and he was a prosperous man; and he was in the house of his master the Egyptian. And his master saw that the Lord was with him, and that the Lord made all that he did to prosper in his hand. And Joseph found grace in his sight, and he served him: and he made him overseer over his house, and all that he had he put into his hand.

– Genesis 39:2–4

290. Favor, goodwill, good breaks, good opportunities, and open doors are guaranteed to those who continually seek good and right in every area of life. We can impact our own favor!

He that diligently seeketh good procureth favour: but he that seeketh mischief, it shall come unto him.

– Proverbs 11:27

291. When you and I carry out the necessary steps that God puts before us, we are not creating the plan. We are fulfilling the requirements of an existing plan. Faith, obedience, and time equal guaranteed success!

For we are his workmanship, created in Christ Jesus unto good works, which God hath before ordained that we should walk in them.

– Ephesians 2:10

292. No matter how much good there is in the world, and no matter how much bad, the world will never be totally perfect. Therefore, we have to make up our minds to be happy right where we are, by choice.

In every thing give thanks: for this is the will of God in Christ Jesus concerning you.

–1 Thessalonians 5:18

293. Often people misunderstand the personality of God, but the Bible clearly tells us God is good, and His mercy endures forever!

The Lord is merciful and gracious, slow to anger, and plenteous in mercy.

– Psalm 103:8

294. Regardless of the challenge or the conflict in life, you and I must still man-up and do what's right—whether it be for ourselves, our family, our community, or our nation.

Be of good courage, and let us play the men for our people, and for the cities of our God: and the Lord do that which seemeth him good.

−2 Samuel 10:12

295. We all have busy schedules. But, we should take time to dedicate ourselves to worshipping and seeking God often. It will build you up for life and give you wisdom for the day. Make Him first, and build your schedule around Him.

And they stood up in their place, and read in the book of the law of the Lord their God one fourth part of the day; and another fourth part they confessed, and worshipped the Lord their God.

– Nehemiah 9:3

296. The combination of giftedness and diligence equals success. Everyone has gifts. Diligence is a choice.

As every man hath received the gift, even so minister the same one to another, as good stewards of the manifold grace of God.

−1 Peter 4:10

297. You are a vital asset to the human story. You have come into His-story for such a time as this. Do not neglect to discover and fulfill your essential role in God's purpose.

For if thou altogether holdest thy peace at this time, then shall there enlargement and deliverance arise to the Jews from another place; but thou and thy father's house shall be destroyed: and who knoweth whether thou art come to the kingdom for such a time as this?

– Esther 4:14

298. God promotes the qualified.

For promotion cometh neither from the east,
nor from the west, nor from the south. But God is the judge: he putteth down one, and setteth up another.

– Psalm 75:6–7

299. Heeding the voice of experience gives safety. Heeding the voice of revelation crosses boundaries. Heeding the voice of navigation helps us to safely cross boundaries.

Be strong and of a good courage: for unto this people shalt thou divide for an inheritance the land, which I sware unto their fathers to give them. Only be thou strong and very courageous, that thou mayest observe to do according to all the law, which Moses my servant commanded thee: turn not from it to the right hand or to the left, that thou mayest prosper whithersoever thou goest. This book of the law shall not depart out of thy mouth; but thou shalt meditate therein day and night, that thou mayest observe to do according to all that is written therein: for then thou shalt make thy way prosperous, and then thou shalt have good success.

– Joshua 1:6–8

300. The joyful expectation of the righteous shall be gladness. The reward of fulfilling God's steps for living will always be gladness!

The hope of the righteous shall be gladness:
but the expectation of the wicked shall perish.

– Proverbs 10:28

301. Mothers are nurturers of destiny. Every mother has the responsibility to nurture the destiny of her child. You are raising a deliverer in society!

And the angel of the Lord appeared unto the woman, and said unto her, Behold now, thou art barren, and bearest not: but thou shalt conceive, and bear a son. Now therefore beware, I pray thee, and drink not wine nor strong drink, and eat not any unclean thing: for, lo, thou shalt conceive, and bear a son; and no razor shall come on his head: for the child shall be a Nazarite unto God from the womb: and he shall begin to deliver Israel out of the hand of the Philistines.

– Judges 13:3–5

302. Victory over all opposition is yours today! You deserve the best that God has to offer today! All that God offers us is good and perfect. Choose life today! Accept the gift of eternal life that God offers us through the Lord Jesus Christ today! Salvation is the key to victory and satisfaction in life today!

Every good gift and every perfect gift is from above, and cometh down from the Father of lights, with whom is no variableness, neither shadow of turning.

– James 1:17

303. Choosing to love one another is the greater part of love; everything else is additional. Love is a choice. Marriage is a commitment.

Many waters cannot quench love, neither can the floods drown it: if a man would give all the substance of his house for love, it would utterly be contemned.

– Song of Solomon 8:7

304. God will give us work in our area of natural talent and skill, through which we are able to provide for ourselves and family and meet the needs of His kingdom, which is saving and serving other people.

Fear not, little flock; for it is your Father's good pleasure to give you the kingdom.
Sell that ye have, and give alms; provide yourselves bags which wax not old, a treasure in the heavens that faileth not, where no thief approacheth, neither moth corrupteth.

– Luke 12:32–33

305. God will prosper you as you receive His Word. His first word to you is that He loves you! His next word is that He wishes above all things that you prosper and be in good health, even as your soul prospers, through obeying the principles of His Word.

Beloved, I wish above all things that thou mayest prosper and be in health, even as thy soul prospereth.

−3 John 1:2

306. In all creation there is profit. Labor is to shape, fashion, make, form, stretch into shape, to worship or increase worth or count worthy.
In all labor or creation or creativity there is preeminence
In all creativity there is abundance
In all creativity there is superiority
In all creativity there is profit
In all labor there is plenty
In all creativity there is plenteousness
In all creativity and craftsmanship there is excellence and opportunity for abundance and more than enough profit.

In all labour there is profit: but the talk of the lips tendeth only to penury.

− Proverbs 14:23

307. Focus only on people, places, events, activities, and thoughts that bring benefit or profit. Invest your time and attention only on that which bring a benefit.

The thoughts of the diligent tend only to plenteousness; but of every one that is hasty only to want.

− Proverbs 21:5

308. Continue to succeed. It makes God happy!

Let them shout for joy, and be glad, that favor My righteous cause: yea, let them say continually, Let The Lord be Magnified, which has pleasure in the prosperity of His servant

– Psalm 35:27

309. See yourself as a diligent, successful person. Prophesy your own future with your words. Call yourself the success you desire to be and you will be transformed into it. You will stand before kings. You will not dwell in the common or mediocre.

Seest thou a man diligent in his business? He shall stand before kings; he shall not stand before mean men

– Proverbs 22:29

310. In order to increase in success in life and achieve uncommon goals, you must increase in wisdom, knowledge, and understanding. Buy and read books. Go to seminars. Buy audio teachings. Value it and you will increase in value.

Buy the truth, and sell it not; also wisdom, and instruction, and understanding.

– Proverbs 23:23

311. Through wisdom a strong home and family is built. By learning to understand one another the home is made stable. However, by increasing in knowledge will the home be filled with wealth and riches.

Through wisdom is a house built: and by understanding it is established:
And by knowledge shall the chambers be filled with all precious and pleasant riches.

– Proverbs 24:3–4

312. Measure not the value of your day in hours; measure your day by the value of your GDP (gross daily product).

Boast not yourself of tomorrow; for you know not what a day may bring forth.

– Proverbs 27:1

313. Useful friendships should make you better, sharper, and more equipped to be effective in life. We all have the ability to bring change in the life of those we are in relationship with, for better or worse.

Iron sharpeneth iron: so a man sharpeneth the countenance of his friend.

– Proverbs 27:17

314. Only the wise appreciate wisdom.

The full soul loatheth an honeycomb; but to the hungry soul every bitter thing is sweet.

– Proverbs 27:7

315. The person who spends time cultivating his or her own mind, gifts, talents, and skills will become prosperous. The person who spends time with useless endeavors and people will experience poverty.

He that tilleth his own land shall have plenty of bread: but he that followeth vain persons shall have poverty enough.

– Proverbs 28:19

316. When people have no goals or vision for life, they lose restraint concerning time, eating habits, exercise, etc. But through a clear vision and discipline success is obtained and thereby happiness.

Where there is no vision, the people perish: but he that keeps the law, happy is he.

– Proverbs 29:18

317. Preparation time is never wasted time, even when others don't understand or approve of your process. Your wisdom will be proven when the winter of life comes.

There be four things which are little upon earth, but they are exceeding wise: The ants are a people not strong, yet they prepare their meat in the summer.

– Proverbs 30: 24–25

318. A virtuous woman is a source of strength, power, increased efficiency, and wealth for her husband. Her value exceeds that of earthly treasure.

Who can find a virtuous woman? For her price is far above rubies. The heart of her husband does safely trust in her, so that he shall have no need of spoil.

– Proverbs 31: 10–11

319. You know you are in a peaceful, quiet environment, when you can hear the echo of your own thoughts in the room.

Better is a dry morsel, and quietness therewith, than an house full of sacrifices with strife.

– Proverbs 17:1

320. Humility is reality. It is walking in understanding of who God is, who you are, and who others are. It is simply walking in a realistic view of your relation with each. We should submit ourselves to God as our Father and Creator. We should love and respect ourselves as His creation. We should love and honor our fellow man as God's creation.

The rich and poor meet together: the Lord is the maker of them all.

– Proverbs 22:2

321. Be champions everyday! And bring it all the time!

—Russell Wilson
Seattle Seahawks, quarterback
2014 NFL Super Bowl XLVIII Champions

Be of good courage, and let us play the men for our people, and for the cities of our God: and The Lord do that which seems Him good.

–2 Samuel 11:12

322. Let your desire be satisfied in your own spouse and not in another. Let only her love satisfy the thirst of your body and soul.

Drink waters out of your own cistern, and running waters out of your own well. Let her be as the loving deer and the pleasant roe; let

her breasts satisfy you at all times; and be ravished always with her love.

– Proverbs 5:15,19

323. Those that are wise enough to take responsibility and initiative for their own lives do not need a boss, ruler, guide, or alarm clock to tell them to prepare for their future.

Go to the ant, thou sluggard; consider her ways and be wise: Which having no guide, overseer, or ruler; provides her meat in the summer and gathers her food in the harvest.

– Proverbs 6:6–8

324. The evidence of what you have truly learned in life, and how you have applied that wisdom, will be shown by the accumulation of results at the end of your life.

The ransom of a man's life are his riches: but the poor hears not rebuke.

– Proverbs 13:7

325. A good student of life leaves a deep scar on the back of the desk of life, that says: "I was here!" The knife they use is results.

The ransom of a man's life are his riches: but the poor hears not rebuke.

– Proverbs 13:7

326. The key to a loving, comfortable, happy, restorative home is the woman of the house. A loving, wise woman makes a house a home. As the husband truly loves the wife, she will build him up and the home.

Every wise woman builds up her house: but the foolish plucketh it down with her hands.

– Proverbs 14:1

327. The Bible gives us an example of love at first sight and leave and cleave in the story of Isaac and Rebekah. This is biblical "falling in love" and marriage.

And Rebekah lifted up her eyes, and when she saw Isaac, she lighted off the camel. For she had said unto the servant, What man is this that walketh in the field to meet us? And the servant had said, It is my master: therefore she took a veil, and covered herself. And the servant told Isaac all things he had done.
And Isaac brought her into his mother Sarah's tent, and took Rebekah, and she became his wife; and he loved her: and Isaac was comforted after his mother's death.

– Genesis 24:64–67

328. Details are the difference between the bronze, the silver, and the gold. It's true in the Olympics, and it's true in life.

Seest thou a man diligent in his business? he shall stand before kings; he shall not stand before mean men.

– Proverbs 22:29

329. You don't get perfect so you can get in school. You get in school so you can get perfected.

Give instruction to a wise man, and he will be yet wiser: teach a just man and he will increase in learning.

— Proverbs 9:9

330. The wise old owl may stare for hours to catch his prey, but he rarely misses!

The heart of the righteous studies to answer: but the mouth of the wicked pours out evil things

— Proverbs 15:28

331. Those who go the extra mile will go the extra mile, and the extra mile wins the race.

Seest thou a man diligent in his business? he shall stand before kings; he shall not stand before mean men.

— Proverbs 22:29

332. Fear is all that stands in the face of the righteous doing exploits of faith.

The wicked flee when no man pursueth: but the righteous are bold as a lion.

— Proverbs 28:1

333. Through humility, we position ourselves as a clear pipeline for the love of God to flow through unhindered by pride.

If a man therefore purge himself from these, he shall be a vessel unto honor, sanctified, and meet for the master's use, and prepared unto every good work.

–2 Timothy 2:21

334. When the stakes get higher, just hit harder!

—Serena Williams
US Open August 27, 2014

Wherefore take unto you the whole armour of God, that ye may be able to withstand in the evil day, and having done all, to stand.

– Ephesians 6:13

335. There are things that God wants to show you of His goodness that will require a long life for you to see. Plan to live until you are completely satisfied. God has wonderful things in store for you.

With long life will I satisfy him,
and shew him my salvation.

– Psalm 91:16

336. New rocket science weight loss program!

Decreased eating plus increased activity equals decreased body weight!

No products to buy! Try it free today!
But wait! There's more! If you double your activity, you can lose almost twice the weight!
Don't wait! Try it today!

But I keep under my body, and bring it into subjection: lest that by any means, when I have preached to others, I myself should be a castaway.

−1 Corinthians 9:27

337. One of the most distinguishing virtues that a woman can have is discretion. Discretion exceeds the value of even beauty as an entry point among greatness, and it certainly ensures a more permanent position.

Many daughters have done virtuously, but thou excellest them all. Favour is deceitful, and beauty is vain: but a woman that feareth the Lord, she shall be praised. Give her of the fruit of her hands; and let her own works praise her in the gates.

− Proverbs 31:29−31

338. Fullness of life is found in following after God as your Father and fulfilling His commandments. The commandments of God are good; they will lead to life, health, peace, happiness, joy, and prosperity. They are the only key to eternal salvation.

For this is the love of God, that we keep his commandments: and his commandments are not grievous.

−1 John 5:3

339. Often God gives you enough to satisfy your thirsty places first, before you receive your abundance.

And the word of the Lord came unto him, saying, Arise, get thee to Zarephath, which belongeth to Zidon, and dwell there: behold, I have commanded a widow woman there to sustain thee. So he arose and went to Zarephath. And when he came to the gate of the city, behold, the widow woman was there gathering of sticks: and he called to her, and said, Fetch me, I pray thee, a little water in a vessel, that I may drink. And as she was going to fetch it, he called to her, and said, Bring me, I pray thee, a morsel of bread in thine hand. And she said, As the Lord thy God liveth, I have not a cake, but an handful of meal in a barrel, and a little oil in a cruse: and, behold, I am gathering two sticks, that I may go in and dress it for me and my son, that we may eat it, and die. And Elijah said unto her, Fear not; go and do as thou hast said: but make me thereof a little cake first, and bring it unto me, and after make for thee and for thy son. For thus saith the Lord God of Israel, The barrel of meal shall not waste, neither shall the cruse of oil fail, until the day that the Lord sendeth rain upon the earth. And she went and did according to the saying of Elijah: and she, and he, and her house, did eat many days.

—1 Kings 17:8–15

340. Do not fear today. Put your trust in the Lord, and call on Him as your Savior; He will protect you and your family from the dangers in the world. He is your rock and protection. Trust in Him today!

Thou shalt not be afraid for the terror by night; nor for the arrow that flieth by day;
nor for the pestilence that walketh in darkness; nor for the destruction that wasteth at noonday. A thousand shall fall at thy side,
and ten thousand at thy right hand;

but it shall not come nigh thee. Only with thine eyes shalt thou behold and see the reward of the wicked. Because thou hast made the Lord, which is my refuge, even the most High, thy habitation; there shall no evil befall thee,
neither shall any plague come nigh thy dwelling. For he shall give his angels charge over thee, to keep thee in all thy ways.
They shall bear thee up in their hands,
lest thou dash thy foot against a stone.

– Psalm 91:5–12

341. You must be bold like a rich man in order to get what you want out of life. Life doesn't yield to the timid.

Joseph of Arimathæa, an honourable counsellor, which also waited for the kingdom of God, came, and went in boldly unto Pilate, and craved the body of Jesus.

– Mark 15:43

342. If you are prospering and thriving in life now, be sure to be thankful and enjoy life to the full. If you are going through a season of difficult challenge, be sure to press into God for comfort. At the end of the day, God has allowed both for the end result that you may trust, love, and know Him only.

In the day of prosperity be joyful, but in the day of adversity consider: God also hath set the one over against the other, to the end that man should find nothing after him.

– Ecclesiastes 7:14

343. Change begins now! Take control of your future today!

Whatsoever thy hand findeth to do, do it with thy might; for there is no work, nor device, nor knowledge, nor wisdom, in the grave, whither thou goest.

– Ecclesiastes 9:10

344. In each learning moment, it is our own responsibility to determine what type of ground our hearts are for receptivity to the seed of the Word sown. We must continually cultivate our own hearts to receive good seed into good ground and bring forth a bountiful harvest in the process of time.

The sower soweth the word. And these are they which are sown on good ground; such as hear the word, and receive it, and bring forth fruit, some thirtyfold, some sixty, and some an hundred.

– Mark 4:14, 20

345. Live daily before an audience of One, and daily you will bless many. Only God knows the true intentions of your heart, whether good or bad. If we seek to please Him by His grace, we will always be successful in His sight. God, our heavenly Father, always decides in our favor. He always believes the best of us. He is always there to give us the grace we need in order to fulfill our responsibility to Him. In doing so, we will fulfill our responsibility to others. And that's all that can truly be asked for.

For the word of God is quick, and powerful, and sharper than any twoedged sword, piercing even to the dividing asunder of soul and

spirit, and of the joints and marrow, and is a discerner of the thoughts and intents of the heart. Neither is there any creature that is not manifest in his sight: but all things are naked and opened unto the eyes of him with whom we have to do. Seeing then that we have a great high priest, that is passed into the heavens, Jesus the Son of God, let us hold fast our profession. For we have not an high priest which cannot be touched with the feeling of our infirmities; but was in all points tempted like as we are, yet without sin. Let us therefore come boldly unto the throne of grace, that we may obtain mercy, and find grace to help in time of need.

– Hebrews 4:12–16

346. Imagine a dream that's larger than life; then grow into your dream!

For with God nothing shall be impossible.

– Luke 1:37

347. The only way that the outside world can recognize your faith in the dark is through your words and actions.

Yea, a man may say, Thou hast faith, and I have works: shew me thy faith without thy works, and I will shew thee my faith by my works.

– James 2:18

348. Truth is what sets us free to live the life God created us to live. He wishes above all things that we prosper, be in good health, even as our mind, will, emotions, and personality matures and prospers. Only truth will allow that to happen.

Then said Jesus to those Jews which believed on him, If ye continue in my word, then are ye my disciples indeed; and ye shall know the truth, and the truth shall make you free.

– John 8:31–32

349. Whatever may be your challenge today, you are well able to overcome and take it on! You were custom-made for your particular challenge in life. You are fully equipped to triumph over every opposition and to maximize every opportunity!

Now thanks be unto God, which always causeth us to triumph in Christ, and maketh manifest the savour of his knowledge by us in every place.

–2 Corinthians 2:14

350. I say unto you that you are a person of prosperity. I decree that peace will be upon you, peace be upon your family and home, and peace and prosperity be upon all that you have on every side. In Jesus name, amen. Accept it by faith!

And thus shall ye say to him that liveth in prosperity, Peace be both to thee, and peace be to thine house, and peace be unto all that thou hast.

–1 Samuel 25:6

351. The government of the world is upon the shoulders of the King of Kings and the Lord of Lords—Jesus Christ. He is quite capable of handling disruptive behavior of the occupants of His kingdom. He is in control. His reign is sovereign. His rule is total. His timing is perfect.

For unto us a child is born, unto us a son is given: and the government shall be upon his shoulder: and his name shall be called Wonderful, Counsellor, The mighty God, The everlasting Father, The Prince of Peace.

Isaiah 9:6

352. Take time to consider the many blessings and benefits God has already given you, and choose to praise the Lord and be thankful. Be assured that the future He has planned for you is even more blessed and fulfilling.

Bless the Lord, O my soul: and all that is within me, bless his holy name. Bless the Lord, O my soul, and forget not all his benefits:

– Psalm 103:1–2

353. As we daily pursue the activities of life, advancement, and progress, may we all be encouraged and determined to pursue to the end. God has a blessing in store for those who serve Him in righteousness. You will be rewarded.

Be ye strong therefore, and let not your hands be weak: for your work shall be rewarded.

–2 Chronicles 15:7

354. Knowledge is the bridge between you and prosperity. The drawbridge is down; we must only put forth the effort and take the time to cross it.

Through wisdom is an house builded; and by understanding it is established: and by knowledge shall the chambers be filled with all precious and pleasant riches.

– Proverbs 24:3–4

355. The Lord is with you today. He is powerful and well able to help and keep you. He loves and celebrates having a child like you. He is committed in His love to you. You are the song on His lips.

The Lord thy God in the midst of thee is mighty; he will save, he will rejoice over thee with joy; he will rest in his love, he will joy over thee with singing.

–Zephaniah 3:17

356. Get ready to embrace yourself because you are larger than you know!

Then he answered and spake unto me, saying, This is the word of the Lord unto Zerubbabel, saying, Not by might, nor by power, but by my spirit, saith the Lord of hosts. Who art thou, O great mountain? before Zerubbabel thou shalt become a plain: and he shall bring forth the headstone thereof with shoutings, crying, Grace, grace unto it.

– Zechariah 4:6–7

357. Whatever may be your task today, work at it heartily, as something done for the Lord, knowing for sure that you will be rewarded and promoted in time.

And whatsoever ye do, do it heartily, as to the Lord, and not unto men; knowing that of the Lord ye shall receive the reward of the inheritance: for ye serve the Lord Christ.

– Colossians 3:23–24

358. Don't be afraid to shine in life! You were made to shine! Just like God made stars in the heaven, He also made "stars" on earth!

Ye are the light of the world. A city that is set on an hill cannot be hid. Neither do men light a candle, and put it under a bushel, but on a candlestick; and it giveth light unto all that are in the house. Let your light so shine before men, that they may see your good works, and glorify your Father which is in heaven.

– Matthew 5:14–16

359. Do not think or speak poverty.
　　　Do not think or speak sickness.
　　　Do not think or speak weakness.
　　　Do not think or speak failure.
　　　Do not think or speak fear.
　　　Do not invite them to your party of life!

Beat your plowshares into swords, and your pruninghooks into spears: let the weak say, I am strong.

– Joel 3:10

360. The key to having more is to use what you already have. If you successfully maximize what you have, more will be added to you.

For the kingdom of heaven is as a man travelling into a far country, who called his own servants, and delivered unto them his goods. And unto one he gave five talents, to another two, and to another one; to every man according to his several ability; and straightway took his journey. Then he that had received the five talents went and traded with the same, and made them other five talents. And

likewise he that had received two, he also gained other two. But he that had received one went and digged in the earth, and hid his lord's money. After a long time the lord of those servants cometh, and reckoneth with them. And so he that had received five talents came and brought other five talents, saying, Lord, thou deliveredst unto me five talents: behold, I have gained beside them five talents more.

His lord said unto him, Well done, thou good and faithful servant: thou hast been faithful over a few things, I will make thee ruler over many things: enter thou into the joy of thy lord. He also that had received two talents came and said, Lord, thou deliveredst unto me two talents: behold, I have gained two other talents beside them. His lord said unto him, Well done, good and faithful servant; thou hast been faithful over a few things, I will make thee ruler over many things: enter thou into the joy of thy lord. Then he which had received the one talent came and said, Lord, I knew thee that thou art an hard man, reaping where thou hast not sown, and gathering where thou hast not strawed: and I was afraid, and went and hid thy talent in the earth: lo, there thou hast that is thine. His lord answered and said unto him, Thou wicked and slothful servant, thou knewest that I reap where I sowed not, and gather where I have not strawed: thou oughtest therefore to have put my money to the exchangers, and then at my coming I should have received mine own with usury. Take therefore the talent from him, and give it unto him which hath ten talents. For unto every one that hath shall be given, and he shall have abundance: but from him that hath not shall be taken away even that which he hath.

– Matthew 25:14–29

361. May the times of war and sacrifice lead us to a time of greater peace, security, and prosperity—in honor of those who served and those who yet serve.

To every thing there is a season,
and a time to every purpose under the heaven:
a time to be born, and a time to die;
a time to plant, and a time to pluck up that which is planted;
a time to kill, and a time to heal;
a time to break down, and a time to build up;
a time to weep, and a time to laugh;
a time to mourn, and a time to dance; a time to cast away stones,
and a time to gather stones together;
a time to embrace, and a time to refrain from embracing;
a time to get, and a time to lose;
a time to keep, and a time to cast away;
a time to rend, and a time to sew;
a time to keep silence, and a time to speak;
a time to love, and a time to hate;
a time of war, and a time of peace.

– Ecclesiastes 3:1–8

362. When nations refuse to submit to the laws of the King of Kings and Lord of Lords, Jesus Christ, they enter into lawlessness, and begin to do what is right in their own eyes, calling right wrong and wrong right, and begin to suffer the consequences.

In those days there was no king in Israel, but every man did that which was right in his own eyes.

– Judges 17:6

363. You are well able to possess the land! No matter what giants may stand in the way of you possessing your promised land! Go in at once and possess it!

And they told him, and said, We came unto the land whither thou sentest us, and surely it floweth with milk and honey; and this is the fruit of it. Nevertheless the people be strong that dwell in the land, and the cities are walled, and very great: and moreover we saw the children of Anak there. The Amalekites dwell in the land of the south: and the Hittites, and the Jebusites, and the Amorites, dwell in the mountains: and the Canaanites dwell by the sea, and by the coast of Jordan. And Caleb stilled the people before Moses, and said, Let us go up at once, and possess it; for we are well able to overcome it.

– Numbers 13:27–30

364. The key to getting paid is to get good! Whatever you are pursuing, get good! Whatever you are doing, get good! Whatever you are wanting, get good! Becoming good at what you do is the key to your success and reward in life.

Seest thou a man diligent in his business? he shall stand before kings; he shall not stand before mean men.

– Proverbs 22:29

365. When you are a person of great destiny, you must associate with others of similar purpose. Greatness sharpens greatness. You make one another better, and you understand the concerns of each other.

Iron sharpeneth iron; so a man sharpeneth the countenance of his friend.

– Proverbs 27:17

366. The Lord has been looking for you. He needs someone with enough faith to believe, even when the miracle is still

small. He needs someone with enough faith and endurance to develop the dream to the end. You will see it come to pass! You will celebrate the fulfillment of your dream!

For the eyes of the Lord run to and fro throughout the whole earth, to shew himself strong in the behalf of them whose heart is perfect toward him. Herein thou hast done foolishly: therefore from henceforth thou shalt have wars.

–2 Chronicles 16:9

367. It takes the anointing to destroy the yoke of the spirit of poverty, but it takes gaining knowledge to show you what to do afterward to become rich.

Through wisdom is an house builded; and by understanding it is established: and by knowledge shall the chambers be filled with all precious and pleasant riches.

– Proverbs 24:3–4

368. The reason you do not have any money is not lack of ability; it's simply because you haven't taken time to sincerely find out how.

Through desire a man, having separated himself, seeketh and intermeddleth with all wisdom.

– Proverbs 18:1

369. The key foundation stone to prospering, achievement, and forward progress is to renew your mind to who God says you are. You can't move forward with low self-esteem. You must believe to achieve!

Beloved, I wish above all things that thou mayest prosper and be in health, even as thy soul prospereth.

–3 John 1:2

370. Let our prayers and intercession be for the families affected by severe weather. The prayers of the righteous avails much for those hurting. Pray for the protection of our nation and the nations of the world.

If my people, which are called by my name, shall humble themselves, and pray, and seek my face, and turn from their wicked ways; then will I hear from heaven, and will forgive their sin, and will heal their land.

–2 Chronicles 7:14

371. There is never any reason to be afraid of another person. People are made of flesh and blood, just like you and I. We are all fragile beings, dependent on a merciful God for life. And there are laws to deal with the lawless.

The Lord is on my side; I will not fear: what can man do unto me? The Lord taketh my part with them that help me: therefore shall I see my desire upon them that hate me.

– Psalm 118:6–7

372. If you want a good future, you must fight for it everyday in your choices of eating habits, exercise, spending, saving, investing, forgiving, planning, loving others, giving, and dreaming. The quality of your future is dependent on today's choices.

Where there is no vision, the people perish: but he that keepeth the law, happy is he.

– Proverbs 29:18

373. Dreams are the things that reality is made of; therefore, we have to dream and work.

For a dream cometh through the multitude of business; and a fool's voice is known by multitude of words.

– Ecclesiastes 5:3

374. May you be celebrated, appreciated, and abundantly compensated for your gifts, talents, and unique contribution to life. In Jesus name, amen!

Be ye strong therefore, and let not your hands be weak: for your work shall be rewarded.

–2 Chronicles 15:7

375. As we prepare to enter into a new week after spending a day worshipping God this Sunday, may the thing that people clearly recognize and perceive about you and me above everything else is that we have been with Jesus Christ, the only begotten Son of God!

Now when they saw the boldness of Peter and John, and perceived that they were unlearned and ignorant men, they marvelled; and they took knowledge of them, that they had been with Jesus.

– Acts 4:13

376. You and I have to make our life and time count everyday. Whether we are blessed to have a relatively long life or a typical life span, we have to believe God to bless and prosper the work of our hands and ask Him to place His favor on all that we do.

And the Lord said, My spirit shall not always strive with man, for that he also is flesh: yet his days shall be an hundred and twenty years.

– Genesis 6:3

377. Singing praise and worship music to God each day will impact your level of joy, health, and success during the day. Happy people have more success and enjoyment in life!

A merry heart doeth good like a medicine: but a broken spirit drieth the bones.

– Proverbs 17:22

378. On a cloudy day, put on a bright shirt or blouse and a bright smile to brighten the day of the people that see you.

A merry heart maketh a cheerful countenance: but by sorrow of the heart the spirit is broken.

– Proverbs 15:13

379. The Lord God created men and women to procreate and populate the earth. His desire is for a godly offspring who are raised and nurtured in the knowledge of God.

And did not he make one? Yet had he the residue of the spirit. And wherefore one? That he might seek a godly seed. Therefore take heed to your spirit, and let none deal treacherously against the wife of his youth.

– Malachi 2:15

380. Happiness is found through obeying God's principles of reverencing God; loving and respecting each other; being diligent in the work you were made for; building a better future; growing in wisdom; and helping others. It produces long life, good health, peace, pleasantness, and prosperity.

Happy is the man that findeth wisdom,
and the man that getteth understanding.
For the merchandise of it is better than the merchandise of silver, and the gain thereof than fine gold. She is more precious than rubies: and all the things thou canst desire are not to be compared unto her. Length of days is in her right hand; and in her left hand riches and honour. Her ways are ways of pleasantness, and all her paths are peace. She is a tree of life to them that lay hold upon her: and happy is every one that retaineth her.

– Proverbs 3:13–18

381. Reading makes you aware. Studying gives you understanding. Practicing makes you proficient. Pursuing makes you profitable.
Persevering establishes you. Faithfulness makes you wealthy.

A faithful man shall abound with blessings:
but he that maketh haste to be rich shall not be innocent.

– Proverbs 28:20

382. One essential key to success and reward in life is to always follow up and to always follow through.

The slothful man roasteth not that which he took in hunting: but the substance of a diligent man is precious.

– Proverbs 12:27

383. The reward for excellence may not always come every Friday, but excellence always eventually produces an abundant, enduring reward.

In all labour there is profit: but the talk of the lips tendeth only to penury.

– Proverbs 14:23

384. When faced with conflict and adversity as a believer in the Lord Jesus Christ, know that your life as a believer is not for your comfort; it's for His glory!

For this thing I besought the Lord thrice, that it might depart from me. And he said unto me, My grace is sufficient for thee: for my strength is made perfect in weakness. Most gladly therefore will I rather glory in my infirmities, that the power of Christ may rest upon me.

–2 Corinthians 12:8–9

385. Excellence is the outgrowth of attitude. Perfection is a goal of measurement. We can always choose the former while being guided, directed, and motivated by the latter. Jesus is the measurement of perfection. His grace makes up the difference for us. However, we can all choose our attitude.

Then this Daniel was preferred above the presidents and princes, because an excellent spirit was in him; and the king thought to set him over the whole realm.

– Daniel 6:3

386. A significant gift creates a significant event. People remember significant events, which creates an opportunity for significant influence and contribution into their lives.

A man's gift maketh room for him, and bringeth him before great men.

– Proverbs 18:16

387. With open hearts, we should receive God's Word. His Word is the source of success in life. We must meditate it with the intent of doing it and not just hearing it. That's the key to good success!

This book of the law shall not depart out of thy mouth; but thou shalt meditate therein day and night, that thou mayest observe to do according to all that is written therein: for then thou shalt make thy way prosperous, and then thou shalt have good success.

– Joshua 1:8

388. One of the keys to success and progress in life is to hook up with those who are diligent in a similar craft or skill as you and multiply your work and potential.

After these things Paul departed from Athens, and came to Corinth; and found a certain Jew named Aquila, born in Pontus, lately come from Italy, with his wife Priscilla; (because that Claudius had commanded all Jews to depart from Rome:) and came unto them.

And because he was of the same craft, he abode with them, and wrought: for by their occupation they were tentmakers.

– Acts 18:1–3

389. A key to accelerating the progress and impact of your work is to connect and collaborate with others of similar or complimentary gifts and skills and focusing on synergistic tasks.

After these things Paul departed from Athens, and came to Corinth; and found a certain Jew named Aquila, born in Pontus, lately come from Italy, with his wife Priscilla; (because that Claudius had commanded all Jews to depart from Rome:) and came unto them. And because he was of the same craft, he abode with them, and wrought: for by their occupation they were tentmakers.

– Acts 18:1–3

390. No one is responsible for building you up but you. Yet, you are responsible to build up and add to everyone you come into contact with out of the overflow of the reservoir within you.

But ye, beloved, building up yourselves on your most holy faith, praying in the Holy Ghost, keep yourselves in the love of God, looking for the mercy of our Lord Jesus Christ unto eternal life.

– Jude 1:20–21

391. The name of Jesus is power when you need it! Whosoever calls upon the name of the Lord shall be saved!

But what saith it? The word is nigh thee, even in thy mouth, and in thy heart: that is, the word of faith, which we preach; that if thou

shalt confess with thy mouth the Lord Jesus, and shalt believe in thine heart that God hath raised him from the dead, thou shalt be saved. For with the heart man believeth unto righteousness; and with the mouth confession is made unto salvation. For the scripture saith, Whosoever believeth on him shall not be ashamed. For there is no difference between the Jew and the Greek: for the same Lord over all is rich unto all that call upon him. For whosoever shall call upon the name of the Lord shall be saved.

– Romans 10:8–13

392. A heart trained, a mind renewed, and a spirit redeemed predisposes a mouth to speak right words.

The mouth of the just bringeth forth wisdom:
but the froward tongue shall be cut out.
The lips of the righteous know what is acceptable: but the mouth of the wicked speaketh frowardness.

– Proverbs 10:31–32

393. Our level of preparation will determine our extent of provision. We must maximize the early, strong seasons of life in order to have abundance in the winter. Small, incremental preparations can create massive increase. The wise maximize time and prepare for the future.

There be four things which are little upon the earth, but they are exceeding wise:
the ants are a people not strong, yet they prepare their meat in the summer.

– Proverbs 30:24–25

394. In life, there's the ideal and there's the real. As we strive to bridge the gap between the two, we must have the maturity to accept and work with others and ourselves and allow God's grace and forgiveness to fill in the gap.

Forbearing one another, and forgiving one another, if any man have a quarrel against any: even as Christ forgave you, so also do ye.

– Colossians 3:13

395. Every man, woman, boy, and girl was created in the image and likeness of God, for His glory, to be like God, and to know and love God as our heavenly Father.

And God said, Let us make man in our image, after our likeness: and let them have dominion over the fish of the sea, and over the fowl of the air, and over the cattle, and over all the earth, and over every creeping thing that creepeth upon the earth. So God created man in his own image, in the image of God created he him; male and female created he them. And God blessed them, and God said unto them, Be fruitful, and multiply, and replenish the earth, and subdue it: and have dominion over the fish of the sea, and over the fowl of the air, and over every living thing that moveth upon the earth.

– Genesis 1:26–28

396. Your heart, mind, will, and spirit is your Promised Land. Everything God has for you He's put in you. However, you and I must take time to till and cultivate our land in order to obtain our harvest. We can't afford empty endeavors, activities, or associations.

He that tilleth his land shall be satisfied with bread: but he that followeth vain persons is void of understanding.

– Proverbs 12:11

397. Thank you is always appropriate to the people who support and help us to be or become who God made us to be. Often, the sustainers of a dream or hope are not always seen, yet they are as essential to it coming to pass as the heart is to the life of the body.

But now hath God set the members every one of them in the body, as it hath pleased him. And if they were all one member, where were the body? But now are they many members, yet but one body. And the eye cannot say unto the hand, I have no need of thee: nor again the head to the feet, I have no need of you. Nay, much more those members of the body, which seem to be more feeble, are necessary: and those members of the body, which we think to be less honourable, upon these we bestow more abundant honour; and our uncomely parts have more abundant comeliness. For our comely parts have no need: but God hath tempered the body together, having given more abundant honour to that part which lacked: that there should be no schism in the body; but that the members should have the same care one for another.

–1 Corinthians 12:18–25

398. Confidence and competence are two essential keys to success; they reduce the desperate need of inordinate dependence on outside help. We can all work together, but we each must be complete within ourselves.

But let every man prove his own work, and then shall he have rejoicing in himself alone, and not in another.

– Galatians 6:4

399. You are of distinct and excellent character. You are an example of outstanding qualities in work, speech, and action. God expects the best of you, and you fulfill God's highest expectations! Now fulfill it!

Seest thou a man diligent in his business? he shall stand before kings; he shall not stand before mean men.

– Proverbs 22:29

400. Use your own mind. Think. Figure things out. Plan. Read. Research. Study. Trust your ability to make a good decision. Don't be overly dependent on the opinions of others. You have a mind. Use it. It's the key to wealth and freedom.

But when it pleased God, who separated me from my mother's womb, and called me by his grace, to reveal his Son in me, that I might preach him among the heathen; immediately I conferred not with flesh and blood: neither went I up to Jerusalem to them which were apostles before me; but I went into Arabia, and returned again unto Damascus. Then after three years I went up to Jerusalem to see Peter, and abode with him fifteen days. But other of the apostles saw I none, save James the Lord's brother.

– Galatians 1:15–19

401. Your successes are your greatest marketing campaign. People judge you based on what you can do or have done and not just what you say.

For a dream cometh through the multitude of business; and a fool's voice is known by multitude of words.

— Ecclesiastes 5:3

402. People without goals do not go anywhere. Goals are the key to obtaining the gold in life. Go for the gold! Set goals!

Where there is no vision, the people perish: but he that keepeth the law, happy is he.

— Proverbs 29:18

403. God will sustain sustainers. God will encourage encouragers of life. God will water those who water His garden—those who tend His flock and family.

The liberal soul shall be made fat: and he that watereth shall be watered also himself.

— Proverbs 11:25

404. To overcome evil with good is the only permanent cure to the evil in the world.

Be not overcome of evil, but overcome evil with good.

— Romans 12:21

405. God's way is the only way to successfully navigate the adversities of life. He is love. He is faithful. He is judge. He is order. He is truth. God is perfect.

But I say unto you, Love your enemies, bless them that curse you, do good to them that hate you, and pray for them which despitefully use you, and persecute you; that ye may be the children of your

Father which is in heaven: for he maketh his sun to rise on the evil and on the good, and sendeth rain on the just and on the unjust. For if ye love them which love you, what reward have ye? do not even the publicans the same? And if ye salute your brethren only, what do ye more than others? do not even the publicans so? Be ye therefore perfect, even as your Father which is in heaven is perfect.

– Matthew 5:44–48

406. In spite of the obvious biases, prejudices, hatred, and resulting violent outbreaks in our world, we each as individuals must choose to love each person based on our own individual desire to love all people. Choosing to love each individual can heal the whole.

Ye are the salt of the earth: but if the salt have lost his savour, wherewith shall it be salted? it is thenceforth good for nothing, but to be cast out, and to be trodden under foot of men. Ye are the light of the world. A city that is set on an hill cannot be hid. Neither do men light a candle, and put it under a bushel, but on a candlestick; and it giveth light unto all that are in the house. Let your light so shine before men, that they may see your good works, and glorify your Father which is in heaven.

– Matthew 5:13–16

407. May our prayers continue to be with the families of the saints who were martyred for their faith and race in Charleston, South Carolina on June 17, 2015. May their memory forever be emblazoned upon the conscience of the American tapestry of history.

Precious in the sight of the Lord is the death of his saints.

– Psalm 116:15

408. We all must make an effort to act on life because situations of life are always seeking to act on us. We must choose life or the choices will be made for us.

Whatsoever thy hand findeth to do, do it with thy might; for there is no work, nor device, nor knowledge, nor wisdom, in the grave, whither thou goest.

– Ecclesiastes 9:10

409. Focus is the difference between success and failure.

Keep thy heart with all diligence;
for out of it are the issues of life.
Put away from thee a froward mouth,
and perverse lips put far from thee.
Let thine eyes look right on,
and let thine eyelids look straight before thee.
Ponder the path of thy feet,
and let all thy ways be established.
Turn not to the right hand nor to the left:
remove thy foot from evil.

–Proverbs 4:23–27

410. God is bigger than your faith; He's bigger than your doubt; and He's bigger than your fear. Because you didn't start it, it's not up to you to finish it. Just follow Him and He will get you there.

Being confident of this very thing, that he which hath begun a good work in you will perform it until the day of Jesus Christ:

– Philippians 1:6

411. You are made in the image and likeness of God Almighty! You were created to prosper, succeed, and thrive! God Almighty is your heavenly Father, and He soooo... loves you, today! Now, call on Him today! Say: "Jesus, I believe You are the Son of God. I believe You died on the cross to pay for my sins. I accept Your payment for my sins. I believe God raised You from the dead for my salvation. I now accept and declare You are my Lord and Savior. I choose now to live for You forever. Thank You Lord Jesus. Amen!"

You are now born-again! You are saved! You are a Christian! You are a believer in the Lord Jesus Christ!

For God so loved the world, that he gave his only begotten Son, that whosoever believeth in him should not perish, but have everlasting life. For God sent not his Son into the world to condemn the world; but that the world through him might be saved.

– John 3:16–17

412. A multitude of small, significant movements create the impact of a large gigantic movement. Every movement in a positive direction equals the sum total impact of a great significant movement. Everything counts!

For a dream cometh through the multitude of business; and a fool's voice is known by multitude of words.

– Ecclesiastes 5:3

413. The angels of the Lord are encamped around about the saints of God, and they are watching our behavior. They

inform our heavenly Father of our merits for our next promotion.

This matter is by the decree of the watchers, and the demand by the word of the holy ones: to the intent that the living may know that the most High ruleth in the kingdom of men, and giveth it to whomsoever he will, and setteth up over it the basest of men.

– Daniel 4:17

414. God is a real God for a real world. He's well able to address your real problems with real help and real solutions and with real power and real grace.

Seeing then that we have a great high priest, that is passed into the heavens, Jesus the Son of God, let us hold fast our profession. For we have not an high priest which cannot be touched with the feeling of our infirmities; but was in all points tempted like as we are, yet without sin. Let us therefore come boldly unto the throne of grace, that we may obtain mercy, and find grace to help in time of need.

– Hebrews 4:14–16

415. Excellence is the chief distinction of winners, no matter where you come from. Mediocrity is far too common. You can be black, white, Asian, Hispanic, Native American, Hawaiian, or other; what really matters is that you are good at what you do.

Seest thou a man diligent in his business?
he shall stand before kings; he shall not stand before mean men.

– Proverbs 22:29

416. The just shall live by faith. It's not a blind faith or baseless hope. No, we have a certain faith— a faith based on the certainty of God's unerring, authoritative Word. God preplanned our lives. There is a specific destination. All we have to do is walk it out.

For we are his workmanship, created in Christ Jesus unto good works, which God hath before ordained that we should walk in them.

– Ephesians 2:10

417. As the antichrist system continues to pervade in the Earth, there will be believing Christians who will truly know their God, and will continue to do exploits of faith. The preservation and redemption of the earth is based on the believer.

And such as do wickedly against the covenant shall he corrupt by flatteries: but the people that do know their God shall be strong, and do exploits.

– Daniel 11:32

418. In any desire, dream, accomplishment, or goal, once you remove the mountain of ignorance and fear, nothing shall be impossible to you, and in actuality, they are one in the same.

And Jesus said unto them, Because of your unbelief: for verily I say unto you, If ye have faith as a grain of mustard seed, ye shall say unto this mountain, Remove hence to yonder place; and it shall remove; and nothing shall be impossible unto you. Howbeit this kind goeth not out but by prayer and fasting.

– Matthew 17:20–21

419. We should place our highest expectation and aspiration upon what God promises. I want the best that He promises! Don't you? Let's not settle for less than God's best!

If they obey and serve him, they shall spend their days in prosperity, and their years in pleasures.

– Job 36:11

420. There is only one truly Supreme Court, and God Almighty is the Judge. He is the Creator of all mankind. He is The Author and Finisher of the definition of marriage between one man and one woman only!

And he answered and said unto them, Have ye not read, that he which made them at the beginning made them male and female, and said, For this cause shall a man leave father and mother, and shall cleave to his wife: and they twain shall be one flesh? Wherefore they are no more twain, but one flesh. What therefore God hath joined together, let not man put asunder.

– Matthew 19:4–6

421. No earthly judge can prevent the inevitable divine judgment from almighty God for their audacity to redefine the God-ordained sanctity of marriage.

Every one that is proud in heart is an abomination to the Lord: though hand join in hand, he shall not be unpunished.

– Proverbs 16:5

422. We are called to love all people whether we agree with certain behaviors or not. However, we cannot change and redefine God's laws of right for all to accommodate the lifestyle choices of a few.

These things also belong to the wise.
It is not good to have respect of persons in judgment. He that saith unto the wicked, Thou art righteous; him shall the people curse, nations shall abhor him: but to them that rebuke him shall be delight, and a good blessing shall come upon them. Every man shall kiss his lips that giveth a right answer.

– Proverbs 24:23–26

423. The key to outstanding success rest in time, talent, and a chance. However, the real deciding factor is whether we use and maximize it.

Whatsoever thy hand findeth to do, do it with thy might; for there is no work, nor device, nor knowledge, nor wisdom, in the grave, whither thou goest. I returned, and saw under the sun, that the race is not to the swift, nor the battle to the strong, neither yet bread to the wise, nor yet riches to men of understanding, nor yet favour to men of skill; but time and chance happeneth to them all.

– Ecclesiastes 9:10–11

424. If the reliability of your truth is based on your level of faith, then your foundation is unstable. However, if the strength of your faith is based on the truth of God's Word, your foundation is unmovable and solid regardless of your level of faith.

Therefore whosoever heareth these sayings of mine, and doeth them, I will liken him unto a wise man, which built his house upon a rock: and the rain descended, and the floods came, and the winds blew, and beat upon that house; and it fell not: for it was founded upon a rock. And every one that heareth these sayings of mine, and doeth them not, shall be likened unto a foolish man, which built his house upon the sand: and the rain descended, and the floods came, and the winds blew, and beat upon that house; and it fell: and great was the fall of it.

– Matthew 7:24–27

425. Called out. Separated. Renewed. Refined. Enhanced. Equipped. Deployed. Dispersed. Multiplied. Repeat. Equals change.

Ye are the salt of the earth: but if the salt have lost his savour, wherewith shall it be salted? it is thenceforth good for nothing, but to be cast out, and to be trodden under foot of men. Ye are the light of the world. A city that is set on an hill cannot be hid. Neither do men light a candle, and put it under a bushel, but on a candlestick; and it giveth light unto all that are in the house. Let your light so shine before men, that they may see your good works, and glorify your Father which is in heaven.

– Matthew 5:13–16

426. There is not a lack of money in the earth. There is only a lack of faith to act on God-given wealth-building ideas.

And Jesus said unto them, Because of your unbelief: for verily I say unto you, If ye have faith as a grain of mustard seed, ye shall say unto this mountain, Remove hence to yonder place; and it shall remove; and nothing shall be impossible unto you. Howbeit this kind goeth not out but by prayer and fasting.

– Matthew 17:20–21

427. The peace that passes all understanding is like having tea time in the middle of a tornado! Just relax and maintain the fundamentals of faith.

And there arose a great storm of wind, and the waves beat into the ship, so that it was now full. And he was in the hinder part of the ship, asleep on a pillow: and they awake him, and say unto him, Master, carest thou not that we perish? And he arose, and rebuked the wind, and said unto the sea, Peace, be still. And the wind ceased, and there was a great calm. And he said unto them, Why are ye so fearful? how is it that ye have no faith? And they feared exceedingly, and said one to another, What manner of man is this, that even the wind and the sea obey him?

– Mark 4:37–41

428. By forming the habit of doing more than paid for, you will eventually develop sufficient strength to enable you to remove yourself from any undesirable station in life, and no one can or will desire to stop you.

—Napoleon Hill
The Law Of Success

Seest thou a man diligent in his business?
he shall stand before kings; he shall not stand before mean men.

– Proverbs 22:29

429. To trust in the Lord gives you and me something greater to live for. Trusting in God helps us go forward, even when faced with great adversity, because we know that

trusting God will always lead us to a place of reward and blessing.

I had fainted, unless I had believed to see the goodness of the Lord in the land of the living.
Wait on the Lord: be of good courage, and he shall strengthen thine heart: wait, I say, on the Lord.

– Psalm 27:13–14

430. You may not know all the answers to where you are going on your life's journey. You may not see the entire path. But with every step of faith forward that you take toward God's plan, you are pleasing and delighting His heart! The just shall live by faith, not by sight.

The steps of a good man are ordered by the Lord: and he delighteth in his way.

– Psalm 37:23

431. Call out to God now by the name of His Holy Son, Jesus! Ask Him to come into your heart. Ask Him to be your Savior. He's only a breath away!

For as I passed by, and beheld your devotions, I found an altar with this inscription, TO THE UNKNOWN GOD. Whom therefore ye ignorantly worship, him declare I unto you. God that made the world and all things therein, seeing that he is Lord of heaven and earth, dwelleth not in temples made with hands; neither is worshipped with men's hands, as though he needed any thing, seeing he giveth to all life, and breath, and all things; and hath made of one blood all nations of men for to dwell on all the face of the earth, and hath determined the times before appointed, and the bounds of their habitation; that they should seek the Lord, if haply

they might feel after him, and find him, though he be not far from every one of us: for in him we live, and move, and have our being; as certain also of your own poets have said, For we are also his offspring.

— Acts 17:23-28

432. Live by faith by exercising God's time tested, proven principles of success. You can then believe for miraculous results. Miracles are guaranteed to the diligent!

Seest thou a man diligent in his business?
he shall stand before kings; he shall not stand before mean men.

— Proverbs 22:29

433. Each new promotion is a stretching opportunity; you will be larger at the end of it than you were at the beginning of it.

For promotion cometh neither from the east,
nor from the west, nor from the south.
But God is the judge: he putteth down one, and setteth up another.

— Psalm 75:6-7

434. You must do what's required to obtain what's desired!

Whatsoever thy hand findeth to do, do it with thy might; for there is no work, nor device, nor knowledge, nor wisdom, in the grave, whither thou goest. I returned, and saw under the sun, that the race is not to the swift, nor the battle to the strong, neither yet bread to the wise, nor yet riches to men of understanding, nor yet favour to men of skill; but time and chance happeneth to them all.

– Ecclesiastes 9:10–11

435. Jesus Christ, The only begotten Son of God and King Of Kings, came and died on the cross in our place and rose again to give us liberty and independence from the tyranny of sin. Accept freedom today!

For God so loved the world, that he gave his only begotten Son, that whosoever believeth in him should not perish, but have everlasting life. For God sent not his Son into the world to condemn the world; but that the world through him might be saved

– John 3:16–17

436. It is God's responsibility to give us a purpose and the grace to accomplish it. However, it is our responsibility to do what's necessary to act on that purpose to release the grace to do what's necessary to bring it to pass.

The heaven, even the heavens, are the Lord's:
but the earth hath he given to the children of men.

– Psalm 115:16

437. I'd rather be living by faith and stretching for something than to just be moving along, not doing anything. The just shall live by faith. It's the key to great achievement.

And the Lord answered me, and said,
Write the vision, and make it plain upon tables, that he may run that readeth it.
For the vision is yet for an appointed time,
but at the end it shall speak, and not lie:
though it tarry, wait for it; because it will surely come, it will not

tarry. Behold, his soul which is lifted up is not upright in him: but the just shall live by **his** faith.

– Habakkuk 2:2–4

438. Big ideas plus big action equals big success!

Whatsoever thy hand findeth to do, do it with thy might; for there is no work, nor device, nor knowledge, nor wisdom, in the grave, whither thou goest. I returned, and saw under the sun, that the race is not to the swift, nor the battle to the strong, neither yet bread to the wise, nor yet riches to men of understanding, nor yet favour to men of skill; but time and chance happeneth to them all.

– Ecclesiastes 9:10–11

439. Let the peace of God keep your heart and mind tonight. Rest in His care. Trust in His love for you, your family, your health, and your well-being. Be blessed as you rest in His grace for your daily living.

Rejoice in the Lord alway: and again I say, Rejoice. Let your moderation be known unto all men. The Lord is at hand. Be careful for nothing; but in every thing by prayer and supplication with thanksgiving let your requests be made known unto God. And the peace of God, which passeth all understanding, shall keep your hearts and minds through Christ Jesus. Finally, brethren, whatsoever things are true, whatsoever things are honest, whatsoever things are just, whatsoever things are pure, whatsoever things are lovely, whatsoever things are of good report; if there be any virtue, and if there be any praise, think on these things. Those things, which ye have both learned, and received, and heard, and seen in me, do: and the God of peace shall be with you.

– Philippians 4:4–9

440. To be successful, you must be narrow-minded—focused—and broad-minded— open—at the same time.

Brethren, I count not myself to have apprehended: but this one thing I do, forgetting those things which are behind, and reaching forth unto those things which are before, I press toward the mark for the prize of the high calling of God in Christ Jesus.

– Philippians 3:13–14

And God gave Solomon wisdom and understanding exceeding much, and largeness of heart, even as the sand that is on the sea shore.

–1 Kings 4:29

441. It's been said that a happy wife equals a happy life. Yet furthermore, a happy husband makes for a prosperous life.

Every man also to whom God hath given riches and wealth, and hath given him power to eat thereof, and to take his portion, and to rejoice in his labour; this is the gift of God.

– Ecclesiastes 5:19

442. See it! Believe it! Act on it! See it!

Now faith is the substance of things hoped for, the evidence of things not seen.

– Hebrews 11:1

443. Say it! Say it! Say it! Believe it! Do it!

And Jesus answering saith unto them, Have faith in God. For verily I say unto you, That whosoever shall say unto this mountain, Be thou removed, and be thou cast into the sea; and shall not doubt in his heart, but shall believe that those things which he saith shall come to pass; he shall have whatsoever he saith. Therefore I say unto you, What things soever ye desire, when ye pray, believe that ye receive them, and ye shall have them.

– Mark 11:22–24

444. God has set up key areas in society to give knowledge for success, such as churches, colleges and universities, and libraries. The knowledge is available; we must only take advantage of it.

Wisdom hath builded her house,
she hath hewn out her seven pillars:
she hath killed her beasts;
she hath mingled her wine;
she hath also furnished her table.
She hath sent forth her maidens:
she crieth upon the highest places of the city,
Whoso is simple, let him turn in hither:
as for him that wanteth understanding, she saith to him, Come, eat of my bread, and drink of the wine which I have mingled.
Forsake the foolish, and live; and go in the way of understanding.

–Proverbs 9:1–6

445. Marriage is God's gift to one man and one woman for the ultimate enjoyment of life together and the greatest potential of achievement and productiveness biologically, financially, and spiritually.

Distinguished Wisdom Presents . . . "Living Proverbs"-Vol.1

And God said, Let us make man in our image, after our likeness: and let them have dominion over the fish of the sea, and over the fowl of the air, and over the cattle, and over all the earth, and over every creeping thing that creepeth upon the earth. So God created man in his own image, in the image of God created he him; male and female created he them. And God blessed them, and God said unto them, Be fruitful, and multiply, and replenish the earth, and subdue it: and have dominion over the fish of the sea, and over the fowl of the air, and over every living thing that moveth upon the earth.

– Genesis 1:26–28

And the Lord God said, It is not good that the man should be alone; I will make him an help meet for him.

– Genesis 2:18

And the Lord God caused a deep sleep to fall upon Adam, and he slept: and he took one of his ribs, and closed up the flesh instead thereof; and the rib, which the Lord God had taken from man, made he a woman, and brought her unto the man. And Adam said, This is now bone of my bones, and flesh of my flesh: she shall be called Woman, because she was taken out of Man. Therefore shall a man leave his father and his mother, and shall cleave unto his wife: and they shall be one flesh. And they were both naked, the man and his wife, and were not ashamed.

– Genesis 2:21–25

Through wisdom is an house builded; and by understanding it is established: and by knowledge shall the chambers be filled with all precious and pleasant riches.

– Proverbs 24:3–4

Drink waters out of thine own cistern, and running waters out of thine own well.

Let thy fountains be dispersed abroad, and rivers of waters in the streets.
Let them be only thine own, and not strangers' with thee. Let thy fountain be blessed: and rejoice with the wife of thy youth.
Let her be as the loving hind and pleasant roe;
let her breasts satisfy thee at all times; and be thou ravished always with her love. And why wilt thou, my son, be ravished with a strange woman, and embrace the bosom of a stranger? For the ways of man are before the eyes of the Lord, and he pondereth all his goings. His own iniquities shall take the wicked himself, and he shall be holden with the cords of his sins. He shall die without instruction; and in the greatness of his folly he shall go astray.

– Proverbs 5:15–23

Two are better than one; because they have a good reward for their labour. For if they fall, the one will lift up his fellow: but woe to him that is alone when he falleth; for he hath not another to help him up. Again, if two lie together, then they have heat: but how can one be warm alone? And if one prevail against him, two shall withstand him; and a threefold cord is not quickly broken.

– Ecclesiastes 4:9–12

446. All skillful, progressive, productive work and craftsmanship that is in accordance with your preordained purpose and talents is profitable.

In all labour there is profit: but the talk of the lips tendeth only to penury.

– Proverbs 14:23

447. To live on purpose is the only way to live to full effectiveness. To live on purpose is the only way to give to

full abundance. Only through God can you live on purpose. He's the author of purpose.

For we are his workmanship, created in Christ Jesus unto good works, which God hath before ordained that we should walk in them.

– Ephesians 2:10

448. When you combine native gifts, talents, and instinct with ascertained skill, education, and training, you increase and multiply potential for great success!

See, I have called by name Bezaleel the son of Uri, the son of Hur, of the tribe of Judah: and I have filled him with the spirit of God, in wisdom, and in understanding, and in knowledge, and in all manner of workmanship, to devise cunning works, to work in gold, and in silver, and in brass, and in cutting of stones, to set them, and in carving of timber, to work in all manner of workmanship.

– Exodus 31:2–5

449. Dignify every moment.

So teach us to number our days, that we may apply our hearts unto wisdom.

– Psalm 90:12

Redeeming the time, because the days are evil.

– Ephesians 5:16

450. Your manner of living and your manner of giving will determine the quality, nature, and level of your reward in life.

For he that soweth to his flesh shall of the flesh reap corruption; but he that soweth to the Spirit shall of the Spirit reap life everlasting.

– Galatians 6:8

451. Finish what you started. You will only eventually be paid for what you actually finish.

I have fought a good fight, I have finished my course, I have kept the faith: henceforth there is laid up for me a crown of righteousness, which the Lord, the righteous judge, shall give me at that day: and not to me only, but unto all them also that love his appearing.

−2 Timothy 4:7–8

452. God is committed to your future success. He is dedicated to your final outcome of life, blessing, and favor. He only asks you to be committed and dedicated to Him.

For I know the thoughts that I think toward you, saith the Lord, thoughts of peace, and not of evil, to give you an expected end. Then shall ye call upon me, and ye shall go and pray unto me, and I will hearken unto you. And ye shall seek me, and find me, when ye shall search for me with all your heart.

– Jeremiah 29:11–13

453. Love everybody, and treat them right. That's what God requires of you; that's what He wants us to do.

Jesus said unto him, Thou shalt love the Lord thy God with all thy heart, and with all thy soul, and with all thy mind. This is the first and great commandment. And the second is like unto it, Thou shalt love thy neighbour as thyself. On these two commandments hang all the law and the prophets.

– Matthew 22:37–40

454. A champion in any area is a champion in every area. The same discipline applies.

Seest thou a man diligent in his business?
he shall stand before kings; he shall not stand before mean men.

– Proverbs 22:29

455. It is impossible to sing and give glory to God and to worry at the same time. When we lift our hands and voices to Him in praise, we automatically have to lay down our cares. He can then solve them!

Rejoice in the Lord alway: and again I say, Rejoice. Let your moderation be known unto all men. The Lord is at hand. Be careful for nothing; but in every thing by prayer and supplication with thanksgiving let your requests be made known unto God. And the peace of God, which passeth all understanding, shall keep your hearts and minds through Christ Jesus. Finally, brethren, whatsoever things are true, whatsoever things are honest, whatsoever things are just, whatsoever things are pure, whatsoever things are lovely, whatsoever things are of good report; if there be any virtue, and if there be any praise, think on these things. Those things, which ye have both learned, and received, and heard, and seen in me, do: and the God of peace shall be with you.

– Philippians 4:4–9

456. A hand that's open is open to give and to receive. A hand that's closed is closed from giving or receiving.

There is that scattereth, and yet increaseth;
and there is that withholdeth more than is meet, but it tendeth to poverty.

– Proverbs 11:24

457. If you want a good future, you must sow seed forward. This schedules the harvest for your desired future. The seed includes money, effort, reading, study, practice, and love.

In the morning sow thy seed, and in the evening withhold not thine hand: for thou knowest not whether shall prosper, either this or that, or whether they both shall be alike good.

– Ecclesiastes 11:6

458. As more and more laws of man attempt to contradict and negate God's divine laws, we who love God must cleave closer to Him and His way of living as a matter of sustaining life, liberty, and decency in society.

It is time for thee, Lord, to work:
for they have made void thy law.
Therefore I love thy commandments
above gold; yea, above fine gold.
Therefore I esteem all thy precepts concerning all things to be right;
and I hate every false way. Thy testimonies are wonderful:
therefore doth my soul keep them.
The entrance of thy words giveth light;
it giveth understanding unto the simple.

– Psalm 119:126–130

459. If you are born-again into the image and likeness of God then you are His son or daughter. You are due and worthy of His inheritance of wealth, riches, and success. However, you need His wisdom in order to possess and maximize your inheritance.

Wisdom is good with an inheritance:
and by it there is profit to them that see the sun. For wisdom is a defence, and money is a defence: but the excellency of knowledge is, that wisdom giveth life to them that have it.

– Ecclesiastes 7:11–12

460. If your destiny depended on another person, that would make him or her God. If your destiny included other people, that would make them a part of God's divine plan.

For promotion cometh neither from the east,
nor from the west, nor from the south.
But God is the judge: he putteth down one, and setteth up another.

– Psalm 75:6–7

461. You can schedule the sowing, but you can't schedule the reaping. However, the sowing definitely schedules the reaping.

Give, and it shall be given unto you; good measure, pressed down, and shaken together, and running over, shall men give into your bosom. For with the same measure that ye mete withal it shall be measured to you again.

– Luke 6:38

462. Take time to discern your own value. Never sell yourself short based on someone else's valuation of your worth.

It is naught, it is naught, saith the buyer:
but when he is gone his way, then he boasteth.

– Proverbs 20:14

463. Learn to know yourself as God knows you; see yourself as God sees you; and love yourself as God loves you. And relax, settle down, and accept yourself in that image.

And God said, Let us make man in our image, after our likeness: and let them have dominion over the fish of the sea, and over the fowl of the air, and over the cattle, and over all the earth, and over every creeping thing that creepeth upon the earth. So God created man in his own image, in the image of God created he him; male and female created he them. And God blessed them, and God said unto them, Be fruitful, and multiply, and replenish the earth, and subdue it: and have dominion over the fish of the sea, and over the fowl of the air, and over every living thing that moveth upon the earth.

– Genesis 1:26–28

464. Do not be discouraged! Do not doubt! Do not be dismayed! You certainly soon will see and experience the reward of your salvation, in time. In Jesus name, amen!

Be ye strong therefore, and let not your hands be weak: for your work shall be rewarded.

–2 Chronicles 15:7

465. Look forward to your future while staying focused on today's steps. Excellence today ensures tomorrow's abundant rewards.

The steps of a good man are ordered by the Lord: and he delighteth in his way.

– Psalm 37:23

466. The life of success is about overcoming the typical odds and doing something exceptional. Anyone can give up, but it takes extraordinary effort to overcome.

Be ye strong therefore, and let not your hands be weak: for your work shall be rewarded.

–2 Chronicles 15:7

467. I am not an opportunity seeker; I'm simply passionate about my purpose. And all the opportunities I need are in the framework of my purpose.

For all these things do the nations of the world seek after: and your Father knoweth that ye have need of these things. But rather seek ye the kingdom of God; and all these things shall be added unto you. Fear not, little flock; for it is your Father's good pleasure to give you the kingdom. Sell that ye have, and give alms; provide yourselves bags which wax not old, a treasure in the heavens that faileth not, where no thief approacheth, neither moth corrupteth.

– Luke 12:30–33

468. It takes integrity to be a real man or a real woman and obey God's laws and principles. Yet, it pays full, rich, lifelong rewards of blessing, security, and peace!

Now the days of David drew nigh that he should die; and he charged Solomon his son, saying, I go the way of all the earth: be thou strong therefore, and shew thyself a man; and keep the charge of the Lord thy God, to walk in his ways, to keep his statutes, and his commandments, and his judgments, and his testimonies, as it is written in the law of Moses, that thou mayest prosper in all that thou doest, and whithersoever thou turnest thyself:

–1 Kings 2:1–3

469. Excellence attracts excellence because there are not too many people there.

Because strait is the gate, and narrow is the way, which leadeth unto life, and few there be that find it.

– Matthew 7:14

470. God didn't call preachers because they are perfect; He called them to do a job. As they do that job, they get better, and so does those who listen to them.

Brethren, I count not myself to have apprehended: but this one thing I do, forgetting those things which are behind, and reaching forth unto those things which are before, I press toward the mark for the prize of the high calling of God in Christ Jesus.

– Philippians 3:13–14

471. Everybody talks about wanting success, but just like Dr. Norvel Hayes has often said, "God is a 'show me' God!" Faith without works is dead!

Yea, a man may say, Thou hast faith, and I have works: shew me thy faith without thy works, and I will shew thee my faith by my works.

– James 2:18

472. Accept the best. God desires for us to have the supreme supply of all things!

Charge them that are rich in this world, that they be not highminded, nor trust in uncertain riches, but in the living God, who giveth us richly all things to enjoy.

–1 Timothy 6:17

473. Problems give you the opportunity to flex your muscles. They reveal how strong you already are while making you stronger at the same time.

There hath no temptation taken you but such as is common to man: but God is faithful, who will not suffer you to be tempted above that ye are able; but will with the temptation also make a way to escape, that ye may be able to bear it.

–1 Corinthians 10:13

474. The promises of the Lord Jesus Christ makes me happy that I'm saved because of the reward and to avoid the judgment!

And God shall wipe away all tears from their eyes; and there shall be no more death, neither sorrow, nor crying, neither shall there be any more pain: for the former things are passed away. And he that sat upon the throne said, Behold, I make all things new. And he said unto me, Write: for these words are true and faithful. And he said unto me, It is done. I am Alpha and Omega, the beginning and the end. I will give unto him that is athirst of the fountain of the water of life freely. He that overcometh shall inherit all things; and I will be his God, and he shall be my son. But the fearful, and unbelieving, and the abominable, and murderers, and whoremongers, and sorcerers, and idolaters, and all liars, shall have their part in the lake which burneth with fire and brimstone: which is the second death.

– Revelation 21:4–8

475. We must live to honor God for ourselves in today's society. Every person will be judged according to his or her own works. Each individual will stand or fall based on his or her own righteousness.

The word of the Lord came again to me, saying, Son of man, when the land sinneth against me by trespassing grievously, then will I stretch out mine hand upon it, and will break the staff of the bread thereof, and will send famine upon it, and will cut off man and beast from it: though these three men, Noah, Daniel, and Job, were in it, they should deliver *but* their own souls by their righteousness, saith the Lord God.
If I cause noisome beasts to pass through the land, and they spoil it, so that it be desolate, that no man may pass through because of the beasts: *though* these three men *were* in it, *as* I live, saith the Lord God, they shall deliver neither sons nor daughters; they only shall be delivered, but the land shall be desolate.
Or *if* I bring a sword upon that land, and say, Sword, go through the land; so that I cut off man and beast from it: though these three men *were* in it, *as* I live, saith the Lord God, they shall deliver

neither sons nor daughters, but they only shall be delivered themselves.
Or *if* I send a pestilence into that land, and pour out my fury upon it in blood, to cut off from it man and beast: though Noah, Daniel, and Job, *were* in it, *as* I live, saith the Lord God, they shall deliver neither son nor daughter; they shall *but* deliver their own souls by their righteousness.

– Ezekiel 14:12–20

476. Excellent quality cannot be hidden or truly imitated; it must be developed.

Seest thou a man diligent in his business?
he shall stand before kings; he shall not stand before mean men.

– Proverbs 22:29

477. Do not let the darkness drown out the light in you and your conversation. Praise the light; and overshadow the darkness.

Rejoiceth not in iniquity, but rejoiceth in the truth.

–1 Corinthians 13:6

478. Our prayers can interrupt the judgments our actions have scheduled.

If my people, which are called by my name, shall humble themselves, and pray, and seek my face, and turn from their wicked ways; then will I hear from heaven, and will forgive their sin, and will heal their land.

–2 Chronicles 7:14

479. We should believe God to be rich. It takes a significant chunk of change to make significant change in society.

A feast is made for laughter, and wine maketh merry: but money answereth all *things.*

– Ecclesiastes 10:19

480. Stand up. Stand out. Make a difference.

Ye are the salt of the earth: but if the salt have lost his savour, wherewith shall it be salted? it is thenceforth good for nothing, but to be cast out, and to be trodden under foot of men. Ye are the light of the world. A city that is set on an hill cannot be hid. Neither do men light a candle, and put it under a bushel, but on a candlestick; and it giveth light unto all that are in the house. Let your light so shine before men, that they may see your good works, and glorify your Father which is in heaven.

– Matthew 5:13–16

481. The promises of the Lord Jesus Christ makes me happy that I'm saved because of the reward and to avoid the judgment.

And God shall wipe away all tears from their eyes; and there shall be no more death, neither sorrow, nor crying, neither shall there be any more pain: for the former things are passed away. And he that sat upon the throne said, Behold, I make all things new. And he said unto me, Write: for these words are true and faithful. And he said unto me, It is done. I am Alpha and Omega, the beginning and the end. I will give unto him that is athirst of the fountain of the water of life freely. He that overcometh shall inherit all things; and I will be his God, and he shall be my son. But the fearful, and unbelieving, and the abominable, and murderers, and whoremongers, and

sorcerers, and idolaters, and all liars, shall have their part in the lake which burneth with fire and brimstone: which is the second death.

— Revelation 21:4–8

482. There are many religions by which people can gain discipline; however, there is only one way by which people must be saved and go to heaven. That is only through the blood and name of the Lord Jesus Christ.

Jesus saith unto him, I am the way, the truth, and the life: no man cometh unto the Father, but by me.

— John 14:6

Be it known unto you all, and to all the people of Israel, that by the name of Jesus Christ of Nazareth, whom ye crucified, whom God raised from the dead, *even* by him doth this man stand here before you whole. This is the stone which was set at nought of you builders, which is become the head of the corner. Neither is there salvation in any other: for there is none other name under heaven given among men, whereby we must be saved.

— Acts 4:10–12

483. God may reveal His favor and love to you with a ray of sunshine bursting through the clouds; or a sudden cool or warm breeze passing through the trees; or the brilliant starlight and shining moon in the night. He's simply saying, "I love you!"

The heavens declare the glory of God; and the firmament sheweth his handywork.
Day unto day uttereth speech, and night unto night sheweth knowledge.

There is no speech nor language, where their voice is not heard.
Their line is gone out through all the earth, and their words to the end of the world. In them hath he set a tabernacle for the sun,
Which is as a bridegroom coming out of his chamber, and rejoiceth as a strong man to run a race.
His going forth is from the end of the heaven, and his circuit unto the ends of it: and there is nothing hid from the heat thereof.
The law of the Lord is perfect, converting the soul: the testimony of the Lord is sure, making wise the simple.
The statutes of the Lord are right, rejoicing the heart: the commandment of the Lord is pure, enlightening the eyes.
The fear of the Lord is clean, enduring for ever: the judgments of the Lord are true and righteous altogether.
More to be desired are they than gold, yea, than much fine gold: sweeter also than honey and the honeycomb.
Moreover by them is thy servant warned: and in keeping of them there is great reward.
Who can understand his errors? cleanse thou me from secret faults.
Keep back thy servant also from presumptuous sins; let them not have dominion over me: then shall I be upright, and I shall be innocent from the great transgression.
Let the words of my mouth, and the meditation of my heart, be acceptable in thy sight, O Lord, my strength, and my redeemer.

–Psalm 19

484. Don't worry! God is larger than us all. He sees everything at the same time. He sees the exterior, interior, peripheral, past, present, future, and eternal view. He can handle your problem! Commit it to the Lord. He cares for you!

Commit thy works unto the Lord,
and thy thoughts shall be established.

– Proverbs 16:3

485. Make your own luck by obeying God's principles.

He that diligently seeketh good procureth favour: but he that seeketh mischief, it shall come unto him.

– Proverbs 11:27

486. Many people have preconceived notions of defeat because they have never seen anyone succeed. However, once the mountain of unbelief is removed, nothing shall be impossible unto you!

And Jesus said unto them, Because of your unbelief: for verily I say unto you, If ye have faith as a grain of mustard seed, ye shall say unto this mountain, Remove hence to yonder place; and it shall remove; and nothing shall be impossible unto you. Howbeit this kind goeth not out but by prayer and fasting.

– Matthew 17:20–21

487. What do you call the number one bottled water in the marketplace?

A leader.

The liberal soul shall be made fat:
and he that watereth shall be watered also himself.

– Proverbs 11:25

488. Jesus is still the answer for the world today. He is the Prince of Peace. He desires goodwill for us all. His angels are

working to bring us peace. Sincere prayer activates His power. Call on His name today!

For unto us a child is born, unto us a son is given: and the government shall be upon his shoulder: and his name shall be called Wonderful, Counsellor, The mighty God,
The everlasting Father, The Prince of Peace.

–Isaiah 9:6

For unto you is born this day in the city of David a Saviour, which is Christ the Lord. And this *shall be a* sign unto you; Ye shall find the babe wrapped in swaddling clothes, lying in a manger. And suddenly there was with the angel a multitude of the heavenly host praising God, and saying, Glory to God in the highest, and on earth peace, good will toward men.

– Luke 2:11–14

489. We must put forth effort in order to lay hold of eternal life, which is the God quality of life, with no lack, no sickness, no defeat, and no limits!

Fight the good fight of faith, lay hold on eternal life, whereunto thou art also called, and hast professed a good profession before many witnesses.

–1 Timothy 6:12

490. Conflict is inevitable, and confrontation is often necessary in order to address the issues that require change.

But speaking the truth in love, may grow up into him in all things, which is the head, *even* Christ:

– Ephesians 4:15

491. Take action in faith based on the reliability of truth in spite of the pervasive influence of feelings. Truth always prevails over feelings.

For we walk by faith, not by sight.

–2 Corinthians 5:7

492. If you're afraid to step out, no one will find out what you can do and you will do without!

Seest thou a man diligent in his business?
he shall stand before kings;
he shall not stand before mean men.

– Proverbs 22:29

493. Do not be discouraged as you pursue the promises of God for your health, marriage, family life, or finances. You will soon taste the good fruit of your faith. Keep hope alive! Your harvest is almost here!

Hope deferred maketh the heart sick:
but *when* the desire cometh, *it is* a tree of life.

–Proverbs 13:12

494. God's blessings are like popcorn! Once you get a pop, the blessings don't stop!

Bring ye all the tithes into the storehouse, that there may be meat in mine house, and prove me now herewith, saith the Lord of hosts, if I

will not open you the windows of heaven, and pour you out a blessing, that *there shall* not *be room* enough *to receive it.*

– Malachi 3:10

495. There's no failure in faith. You are pleasing to God if you're living by faith, whether you see all the answers immediately or not.

But without faith it is impossible to please him: for he that cometh to God must believe that he is, and that he is a rewarder of them that diligently seek him.

– Hebrews 11:6

496. We all must live by faith, whether we work for Walmart or on Wall Street. The only sure thing is in pleasing God by faith.

But without faith it is impossible to please him: for he that cometh to God must believe that he is, and that he is a rewarder of them that diligently seek him.

– Hebrews 11:6

497. People who cheat on their marriage covenant cheat themselves out of their inheritance.

I made a covenant with mine eyes; why then should I think upon a maid? For what portion of God is there from above? and what inheritance of the Almighty from on high?

– Job 31:1–2

498. We should take time to honor God at the beginning of the week by giving him singing, worship, tithes and offerings, and reverence to acknowledge our dependence on Him and love for Him.

Bring ye all the tithes into the storehouse, that there may be meat in mine house, and prove me now herewith, saith the Lord of hosts, if I will not open you the windows of heaven, and pour you out a blessing, that there shall not be room enough to receive it.

— Malachi 3:10

499. Missed opportunities are not the end of the world. Yet, seized opportunities can be the beginning of a new world!

Boast not thyself of to morrow;
for thou knowest not what a day may bring forth.

— Proverbs 27:1

500. Eternal words are not restricted to the realm of time. They can speak to you at the right time in any time or generation.

Jesus Christ the same yesterday, and to day, and for ever.

— Hebrews 13:8

501. It's one thing to be "liked" on Facebook; however, it's another thing to be "liked" by God! It's called favor!

Howbeit the Lord God of Israel chose me before all the house of my father to be king over Israel for ever: for he hath chosen Judah to be the ruler; and of the house of Judah, the house of my father; and

among the sons of my father he _**liked**_ me to make me king over all Israel:

–1 Chronicles 28:4

502. Stars have a tendency to gather together into constellations, forming a more meaningful picture.

From whom the whole body fitly joined together and compacted by that which every joint supplieth, according to the effectual working in the measure of every part, maketh increase of the body unto the edifying of itself in love.

– Ephesians 4:16

503. Don't let anyone define your faith for you. Others can influence your faith, but don't let them define it.

We having the same spirit of faith, according as it is written, I believed, and therefore have I spoken; we also believe, and therefore speak.

–2 Corinthians 4:13

504. Excellence has an address. It can be arrived at within the scope of any occupation or endeavor. The path to get there is always by traveling up Diligence Highway.

Because strait is the gate, and narrow is the way, which leadeth unto life, and few there be that find it.

– Matthew 7:14

505. God works with the people who work to fulfill His good pleasure.

But Jesus answered them, My Father worketh hitherto, and I work.

– John 5:17

506. Do not be discouraged. If you have started to seek the Lord and to do his will, He has heard you and He has taken notice. Your blessing, answer, and help are on the way!

Then said he unto me, Fear not, Daniel: for from the first day that thou didst set thine heart to understand, and to chasten thyself before thy God, thy words were heard, and I am come for thy words.

– Daniel 10:12

507. This morning say right now, "I am strong! I am victorious! I am a success! I win! I am loved! In Jesus name, amen!"

A man's belly shall be satisfied with the fruit of his mouth; *and* with the increase of his lips shall he be filled. Death and life *are* in the power of the tongue: and they that love it shall eat the fruit thereof.

– Proverbs 18:20–21

508. Great adventures of faith start with hope. Hope is a desire and joyful expectation of fulfillment based on the reliability of truth. Start your adventure today by believing God's Word—the Bible!

Now faith is the substance of things hoped for, the evidence of things not seen.

– Hebrews 11:1

So then faith cometh by hearing, and hearing by the word of God.

– Romans 10:17

509. Prayer is the heartbeat of a church. It's where we hear God's heart, and it's where God hears ours.

And he spake a parable unto them *to this end*, that men ought always to pray, and not to faint.

– Luke 18:1

510. Thank God today for all the challenges He has helped you overcome, and now know that there is no challenge too great for you to overcome through Him!

For by thee I have run through a troop;
and by my God have I leaped over a wall.

– Psalm 18:29

511. The foundation of our faith is God's Word, not our circumstances. Therefore, as circumstances change for better or worse, do not let your faith fail you. Continue to stand on God's Word.

And Peter answered him and said, Lord, if it be thou, bid me come unto thee on the water. And he said, Come. And when Peter was come down out of the ship, he walked on the water, to go to Jesus. But when he saw the wind boisterous, he was afraid; and beginning to sink, he cried, saying, Lord, save me. And immediately Jesus stretched forth his hand, and caught him, and said unto him, O thou

of little faith, wherefore didst thou doubt? And when they were come into the ship, the wind ceased.

– Matthew 14:28–32

512. Roll your concerns over on the Lord in prayer daily, moment by moment, and your thoughts and plans shall be made straight, plain, and established.

Commit thy works unto the Lord,
and thy thoughts shall be established.

– Proverbs 16:3

513. Even when your circumstances appear to be going out of control, your destiny remains stable and the same. Anchor your soul upon the stability of what God has spoken about your true destiny.

That by two immutable things, in which *it was* impossible for God to lie, we might have a strong consolation, who have fled for refuge to lay hold upon the hope set before us: which *hope* we have as an anchor of the soul, both sure and stedfast, and which entereth into that within the veil.

– Hebrews 6:18–19

514. We often neglect our faith for healing; however, if we use our faith it will not neglect us.

For I am not ashamed of the gospel of Christ: for it is the power of God unto salvation to every one that believeth; to the Jew first, and also to the Greek. For therein is the righteousness of God revealed from faith to faith: as it is written, The just shall live by faith.

– Romans 1:16–17

515. Some would love to have the blessings you complain about everyday. They would love to have that job, house, car, family, etc., which you complain about everyday.

Bless the Lord, O my soul:
and all that is within me, bless his holy name.
Bless the Lord, O my soul,
and forget not all his benefits.

– Psalm 103:1–2

516. The soul seeks wisdom as the earth seeks the rain, knowing that it is the principle thing for life.

Wisdom is the principal thing; therefore get wisdom: and with all thy getting get understanding.

– Proverbs 4:7

517. Evaluate people by their fruit, not by their thorns. Is not a rose beautiful, though it has thorns? Are not blackberries sweet, though they have thistles?

Ye shall know them by their fruits. Do men gather grapes of thorns, or figs of thistles? Even so every good tree bringeth forth good fruit; but a corrupt tree bringeth forth evil fruit. A good tree cannot bring forth evil fruit, neither can a corrupt tree bring forth good fruit. Every tree that bringeth not forth good fruit is hewn down, and cast into the fire. Wherefore by their fruits ye shall know them.

– Matthew 7:16–20

518. An eagle serves no one pecking on the ground with the chickens. An eagle is made to soar and give others something to look up to!

But when it pleased God, who separated me from my mother's womb, and called me by his grace, to reveal his Son in me, that I might preach him among the heathen; immediately I conferred not with flesh and blood: neither went I up to Jerusalem to them which were apostles before me; but I went into Arabia, and returned again unto Damascus. Then after three years I went up to Jerusalem to see Peter, and abode with him fifteen days. But other of the apostles saw I none, save James the Lord's brother.

– Galatians 1:15–19

519. Everyone has sensibilities of greatness. If all people would walk in who they truly are, we all would be truly gods of the earth!

I have said, Ye are gods; and all of you are children of the most High.

– Psalm 82:6

520. When you can't make a decision, be guided by the mission.

I will bless the Lord, who hath given me counsel:
my reins also instruct me in the night seasons.
I have set the Lord always before me:
because *he is* at my right hand, I shall not be moved.

– Psalm 16:7–8

521. Physical life may lasts only so long, yet a transcendent vision can last forever.

Where there is no vision, the people perish:
but he that keepeth the law, happy is he.

– Proverbs 29:18

522. We must live our remaining days on purpose. We must evaluate where we are and maximize our remaining strength

to make the most of our remaining life and influence on earth.

So teach us to number our days,
that we may apply our hearts unto wisdom.

– Psalm 90:12

523. A good husband notices the needs of his wife and remedies them. A good business notices the needs of their customers and supplies them. Excellence is gained by predicting and meeting needs.

Husbands, love your wives, even as Christ also loved the church, and gave himself for it.

– Ephesians 5:25

524. Carve out time each day to reverence and acknowledge God for your life, health, and strength. Seek Him for wisdom. Ask for His help. He will never let you down.

Seek the Lord and his strength,
seek his face continually.

–1 Chronicles 16:11

525. God has certain guidelines for the leaders He chooses. The first of which is that they obey and be guided by His Word. Otherwise, they will abuse their position.

And it shall be, when he sitteth upon the throne of his kingdom, that he shall write him a copy of this law in a book out of *that which is* before the priests the Levites: and it shall be with him, and he shall read therein all the days of his life: that he may learn to fear the Lord his God, to keep all the words of this law and these statutes, to do them: that his heart be not lifted up above his brethren, and that he turn not aside from the commandment, *to the*

right hand, or *to* the left: to the end that he may prolong *his* days in his kingdom, he, and his children, in the midst of Israel.

– Deuteronomy 17:18–20

526. God has a wonderful way of making what initially seemed terrible turn out to be bearable!

There hath no temptation taken you but such as is common to man: but God is faithful, who will not suffer you to be tempted above that ye are able; but will with the temptation also make a way to escape, that ye may be able to bear it.

–1 Corinthians 10:13

527. If you take time to refine yourself, you will find yourself.

And when he was demanded of the Pharisees, when the kingdom of God should come, he answered them and said, The kingdom of God cometh not with observation:
Neither shall they say, Lo here! or, lo there! for, behold, the kingdom of God is within you.

– Luke 17:20–21

528. I believe God is giving us an extension of time. I believe He is giving us another chance. We can make a difference. We can make a change!

But, beloved, be not ignorant of this one thing, that one day *is* with the Lord as a thousand years, and a thousand years as one day. The Lord is not slack concerning his promise, as some men count slackness; but is longsuffering to us–ward, not willing that any should perish, but that all should come to repentance. But the day of the Lord will come as a thief in the night; in the which the heavens

shall pass away with a great noise, and the elements shall melt with fervent heat, the earth also and the works that are therein shall be burned up.

–2 Peter 3:8–10

529. Never regret the trials and test it took to refine the treasure inside of you. Is not the diamond fortunate to have endured the pressure and heat that developed its glistening brilliance?

Beloved, think it not strange concerning the fiery trial which is to try you, as though some strange thing happened unto you:
But rejoice, inasmuch as ye are partakers of Christ's sufferings; that, when his glory shall be revealed, ye may be glad also with exceeding joy.
If ye be reproached for the name of Christ, happy are ye; for the spirit of glory and of God resteth upon you: on their part he is evil spoken of, but on your part he is glorified.
But let none of you suffer as a murderer, or as a thief, or as an evildoer, or as a busybody in other men's matters.
Yet if any man suffer as a Christian, let him not be ashamed; but let him glorify God on this behalf.
For the time is come that judgment must begin at the house of God: and if it first begin at us, what shall the end be of them that obey not the gospel of God?
And if the righteous scarcely be saved, where shall the ungodly and the sinner appear?
Wherefore let them that suffer according to the will of God commit the keeping of their souls to him in well doing, as unto a faithful Creator.

–1 Peter 4:12–19

530. Wisdom is the principal thing. As we seek God, He will give us the wisdom we need to navigate life. He will lead us into prosperity, good health, happiness, and peace. God is love, and God loves you!

I love them that love me; and those that seek me early shall find me.
Riches and honour are with me; yea, durable riches and righteousness.
My fruit is better than gold, yea, than fine gold; and my revenue than choice silver.
I lead in the way of righteousness, in the midst of the paths of judgment:
That I may cause those that love me to inherit substance; and I will fill their treasures.

– Proverbs 8:1

Final Word

You've been enjoying *Distinguished Wisdom Presents: Living Proverbs —Volume 1*. Please continue to read and reread these proverbs and supporting scriptures. You will grow in wisdom, depth, and insight for living your daily life more successfully. Thank you again for taking time to immerse your heart into these *Living Proverbs*. My prayer to God for you is this: *May Your Life Be Enriched By The Words Of Wisdom*

About The Author

Pastor Terrance Levise Turner is the senior pastor of Faith Country Holiness Church in Gallatin, TN. Pastor Turner has an MBA in Finance and Supply Chain Management from Tennessee State University. He also has a bachelor's of Speech Communications and Theater, with a concentration in mass communications from Tennessee State University. Pastor Turner is the author of several books, including the *"Living Proverbs"* series, and *Your Wealth Is In Your Anointing: Discover Keys To Releasing Your Potential.* His books and audiobooks are available at www.TerranceTurnerBooks.com. Terrance is also a singer/songwriter/recording artist. He ministers the gospel in Word and song with his wife, Avis. Their music is available at www.FaithCountryProductions.com. They live in Nashville, TN. Pastor Turner continues to serve the community and Body of Christ through service, music, and teaching the Word of God.

www.ingramcontent.com/pod-product-compliance
Lightning Source LLC
Chambersburg PA
CBHW020421010526
44118CB00010B/361